6⁴⁹⁵

Diversity Training for Classroom Teaching

A Manual for Students and Educators

Caroline S. Clauss-Ehlers

Diversity Training for Classroom Teaching

A Manual for Students and Educators

 Springer

Author:
Caroline S. Clauss-Ehlers
Rutgers, The State University of New Jersey, U.S.A.

Library of Congress Cataloging-in-Publication Data

A C.I.P. Catalogue record for this book is available
from the Library of Congress.

HC ISBN 10: 0-387-27765-X	ISBN 13: 9780387277653	Printed on acid-free paper.
SC ISBN 10: 0-387-27770-6	ISBN 13: 9780387277707	Printed on acid-free paper.
e-ISBN 10: 0-387-27771-4	eISBN 13: 9780387277714	

Library of Congress Control Number: 2006920017

Printed in the United States of America.

9 8 7 6 5 4 3 2 1

springeronline.com

To all the students whose interest and commitment to diversity in the classroom have shaped the pages that follow.

To my loving husband Julian, our wonderful daughter Isabel Seay, and our newborn daughter, Sabrina Seay, whose magic has just begun to unfold.

Table of Contents

Section 3. Dimensions of Difference: Gender

Section 4. Other Challenges to Diversity

Section 5. Understanding Exceptional Microcultures

Section 6. Conclusion

Foreword

Diversity Training for Classroom Teaching: A Manual for Students and Educators is an excellent guide for preparing responsive teachers, capable of exploring the roots of a wide variety of types of diversity and acting with knowledge and sensitivity to improve student learning and self-efficacy.

Today's educators and future educators are challenged by a student body of increasing diversity. The need to respect and attend to differences through responsive teaching is seen as a key element to student success in school. Attention to diversity has become a top priority in our state departments of education as evidenced in the content standards for teacher preparation of many states. Expectations such as, "Prospective teachers will understand the importance of social, cultural, linguistic, and cognitive differences," are common in standards developed for pre-service teacher education programs.

Addressing increased diversity in today's K-12 education has become a priority at the district, school, and classroom levels, as well. Ironically, many have observed that while student bodies have become increasingly diverse, individuals drawn to teaching are more likely to be from somewhat similar backgrounds - "upper" working class or middle class; Caucasian, good to high achievers; and those who consider themselves to be in the social and cultural mainstream. Some consider the growing 'mismatch' between teachers and students to be problematic. Indeed, a particular teacher's self-perception and self-identity is believed to play an important role in how that teacher will view and respond to differences among others. New teachers, in particular, entering their own classrooms for the first time are apt to be overwhelmed by the variability of the students they have been asked to teach. Needless to say, the differences they encounter (and there are bound to be many) are inevitable. The key is to prepare teachers by encouraging them to understand the nature of differences, including their own personal histories, and empowering them to deal with differences in the classrooms and communities in which they teach.

Unfortunately, support for new teachers to help them meet the varied needs of their students varies considerably from one district to another. Curriculum guides for specific content areas give little or no assistance in helping teachers deal with the multiplicity of demands placed upon them by virtue of the context in which they must teach and students must learn.

Fortunately, efforts at the pre-service level to help teachers feel better equipped to handle these issues have increased in recent years. Most of that effort has been focused on the needs of culturally and linguistically diverse students. This is important and sorely needed. However, the elements of diversity go far beyond the issues of culture and language. Indeed, issues of language and culture are often complicated by other aspects of diversity that must be addressed at home and school.

Diversity Training for Classroom Teaching: A Manual for Students and Educators is unique in its approach to broaden the scope of how we view what is important for teachers to know and be able to do regarding diversity in their classrooms. It does this in a variety of ways that help teachers build a repertoire of knowledge and skills that they can draw upon when needed. Three elements stood out for me. First, teachers are helped to form a point of view toward diversity that transcends specific characteristics or subsets of students. This allows them to embrace differences and approach them with an open mind that fosters the ability to suspend judgment and proceed with fairness and responsiveness. Second, teachers are offered a solid, research-based corpus of information about specific types of diversity. This helps build background knowledge relative to specific dimensions of difference and various exceptional microcultures they are likely to encounter. Finally, teachers are given a wealth of concrete ideas on how to recognize and address particular circumstances in a student's life that may have an impact on the ability to function successfully.

This is an extraordinary volume, useful for pre-service instructors and their students as well as those involved in in-service, ongoing professional development.

In-service teachers and administrators might enter the book at any point of interest and use the information and activities as a basis for rich discussion and the development of action plans. Even the most seasoned teachers will find content that will be useful in their current work and much they wished they had known when they first entered the profession. I commend Caroline S. Clauss-Ehlers for an outstanding contribution to the field.

DOROTHY S. STRICKLAND
Samuel DeWitt Proctor Professor of Education
--Rutgers, The State University of New Jersey

Acknowledgments

Thanks to everyone at Springer, with special thanks to Editor Marie Sheldon who believed in the value of this project from the beginning and helped it become a reality.

A very special mention to Richard De Lisi, whose enthusiasm about this book was contagious.

Many thanks to Dorothy S. Strickland, for her support and knowledge.

For their feedback and encouragement, thanks to Wan-Chun Chen, Ya-Ting Tina Yang, and Antonia Hernandez.

For the sharing of their expertise, feedback, and insight, many thanks to Lawrence A. Kutner and Rafael Art. Javier.

Finally, I thank my growing nuclear family for their heartfelt support, love, and patience. I hope a book like this in some small way creates a more just world for everyone's children.

Section 1

Foundations

Chapter 1

Introduction:
How to Use this Manual

Good teaching is about developing a relationship. It is a relationship between teacher and student as knowledge is shared. It is a relationship that develops among students as they work together to test out concepts and build new knowledge. It is a relationship between students and teachers and the material presented. As minds develop and grow, course material is understood in new and exciting ways. Knowledge builds on itself and new perspectives take shape. Teaching for diversity means the teaching relationship occurs in a classroom where educators are responsive to the diverse needs of all students.

Being aware of your own cultural background is a critical part of being effective with a heterogeneous classroom (Sue, 1998). Unfortunately, many educational systems have functioned without a strong recognition of this multicultural context (Clauss-Ehlers, 2003). The risks of this oversight are profound. Academic and emotional setbacks result when students' unique cultures are not incorporated into the life of the classroom. Without a reflection of themselves in their learning, initially enthusiastic students are likely to feel alienated from the classroom experience.

Diversity Training for Classroom Teaching: A Manual for Students and Educators is designed to help you incorporate the authentic identities of all your students into the practice of teaching. This manual is like a road map, organized to guide you (whether instructor or student) in courses that address issues of diversity in educational settings. *Diversity Training for Classroom Teaching* provides information and skill-building activities that relate to the diverse topics presented. Throughout the book you are encouraged to create your view of successful multicultural education.

This book is also based on the belief that pre-service diversity courses in educational programs play a major role in the way that you will respond to difference in the classroom. This is particularly true given that the pre-service diversity course is usually the first and only diversity class that students take in their undergraduate or graduate careers. *Diversity Training for Classroom Teaching* challenges you to re-examine your belief systems and construct a theory about how you will respond to difference as a future educator. As the text will show, if youth are respected rather than marginalized for their differences, they will thrive in their classrooms, schools, and communities (See Clauss-Ehlers & Weist, 2004). In this sense, *Diversity Training for Classroom Teaching* is a book about forging empathy.

Current policy mandates that pre-service teachers take a course in cultural diversity. As America's classrooms become more demographically diverse, you must learn how to respond to the different needs and cultural styles of diverse children. While many existing textbooks highlight these issues, their focus is often on research and theory. Missing from much of this literature is a practical guide to help you incorporate diversity in the classroom. *Diversity Training for Classroom Teaching* seeks to fill this gap. The pages that follow provide a how-to toolkit where you participate in a multitude of activities and reflective scenarios. The goal of this work is to have you acquire the necessary skills for work in diverse settings.

The *Diversity Training Activities* presented in this book define terminology, raise self-awareness, illustrate the relevance of concepts, and encourage you to engage in a dialogue about diversity. You will develop a repertoire of skills based on an understanding of people's diverse realities and how they play out in educational settings. The purpose of these activities is to help you feel more confident about your ability to take action when youth and their families experience issues like racism, stigma, and language barriers, to name a few.

Each *Diversity Training Activity* is divided into three parts: *Rationale, Steps to Implementation*, and *Discussion Points*. The *Rationale* section spells out the activity's purpose and relevance to the chapter's central theme. The *Steps to Implementation* section walks you through how to carry out the activity. The *Discussion Points* aspect of the activity presents questions designed to facilitate critical classroom discussion.

Diversity Training for Classroom Teaching: A Manual for Students and Educators is divided into six overall sections. The first section, Foundations, provides the necessary groundwork for teaching a diversity course or taking one. This work involves discussing your expectations and assumptions about the course. The Foundations section shows you how to address student concerns while also maintaining the essence of the curriculum. Activities include setting ground rules, exploring how empathy relates to diversity, and defining what is meant by difference.

Sections 2 and 3 build on this general foundation and explore dimensions of difference that include cultural values, socioeconomic status, race, ethnicity, language, and gender. A chapter devoted to building educational partnerships with diverse families is also included.

One of the unique aspects of this manual is that difference is explored broadly. While more traditional concepts of difference like race and gender are discussed, the book moves beyond these to consider other areas that influence children's experience. Section 4 addresses additional challenges to diversity such as bullying, classroom management, child abuse, and how to foster resilience. Section 5 examines different microcultures (i.e., separate cultures organized around a particular experience) that include trauma, eating disorders, and childhood depression. Here you will learn how to recognize warning signs associated with emotional disturbance. Chapter 15, *Exceptional Microcultures: How to Make a Referral*, will introduce you to the referral process and help you think through how to respond to a student in crisis.

The topics presented in Sections 4 and 5 were selected due to the likelihood that educators will deal with them in the K-12 classroom. While many of my education students have said they know how to develop a lesson plan for math or social studies, they are uncertain about how to respond to a student who says he wants to hurt himself, cannot focus, or is experiencing depression. Abilities you will develop as you go through Sections 4 and 5 are: how to cope with a bully at school; how to engage parents in the learning process; how to manage a classroom; how to recognize signs and symptoms associated with depression, trauma, and eating disorders; and how to make a referral.

Section 6, the concluding section of this book, encourages you to reflect on the course. You will be asked to think about what you have learned about yourself, how you define your teaching style, and how you envision your future work as an educator.

Each chapter concludes with *Diversity Training Activities* and note space where you can record your thoughts about concepts and theories, classroom objectives, and best practices. A Web resources section is also provided for each topic. Please note that Website listings are for your information and not necessarily endorsed by the author. All Websites were reviewed in May 2005 to make sure they were still operating.

A glossary of relevant terms is provided as well as a bibliography of selected readings that correspond with each chapter. Appendix A presents a sample course syllabus to use as a model for the course. Appendix B presents an educational intervention proposal outline that students complete as their final course assignment.

Having reviewed the structure of the book, the remainder of this chapter will present three activities for soon-to-be educators. Three issues that often come up for education students studying diversity are:

- The Educational Case for Diversity
- Setting Classroom Ground Rules
- Best and Worst Learning Experiences

DIVERSITY TRAINING ACTIVITY 1.1
THE EDUCATIONAL CASE FOR DIVERSITY

RATIONALE

My experience teaching diversity courses is that education students often come to class wondering why they have to take them. Some students feel resentful about having to enroll in another mandatory class and question the value of a course on diversity. A first step towards student commitment is to acknowledge these feelings. It is important that students feel heard, especially if they're wondering, "If I'm a good teacher and know my basic skill areas, why should this diversity stuff matter? Why can't a math lesson be understood by all students, in the same way, whatever the student's background?" Others assume that school systems are not that diverse, a view that often reflects the individual's own homogeneous school experience. Table 1.1 lists concerns students have shared when faced with taking a course on diversity. It is this discussion that sets the backdrop for the first *Diversity Training Activity*.

Table 1.1 Negative Assumptions About Cross Cultural Courses

Student concerns about taking a diversity course:
1. People may take things the wrong way in this course.
2. Stereotypes may arise in the course and we may not know how to handle them.
3. People may get upset about the different life choices presented in the course.
4. The course may leave out discussion about certain groups.
5. The class may not really be that important and just be given a fancy title.
6. Diversity may be viewed as only a negative issue.
7. Cross-cultural classes do not require any work and just go through the motions.
8. Only one view will be presented in the course.
9. Nothing from the course will be of practical use in an educational setting.
10. Students will feel uncomfortable discussing some topics.
11. A comment will not come out right and my classmates will make wrong assumptions about me.
12. The course will reinforce stereotypes.
13. The course will cover obvious material and just be "fluff."
14. There are no answers to resolve an issue as complex as diversity.
15. The course may address why problems like bullying occur, but students won't learn how to prevent or effectively deal with them. As a result, students won't learn anything that can be applied to their careers as future teachers.
16. The professor will not know how to deal with the problems presented in class unless he or she grew up with them.

STEPS TO IMPLEMENTATION

1. Your instructor will divide the class into small groups of 4 to 5 students each.
2. Consider the following questions in your small group:
   a) How diverse are today's youth in terms of race and ethnicity?
   b) What informs your belief?
   c) How will your belief influence your teaching?
3. Look at Table 1.2 *Demographics of Ethnic Minority Youth* presented below.

Table 1.2 Demographics of Ethnic Minority Youth:
Total percentage* of the U.S. youth population by race in 2000

Year	White (non-Latino)	Black/ African American	American Indian/ Alaska Native	Asian & Asian Amer	Native Hawaiian/ Pacific Islander	Hispanic/ Latino	Two or more races
<1	1.1	1.6	1.7	1.3	1.6	2.2	3.0
1-4	4.6	6.5	6.9	5.3	6.8	8.3	10.9
5-13	11.6	16.5	17.6	12.0	16.3	17.5	20.5
14-17	5.3	6.8	7.7	5.5	7.2	6.9	7.4
Total<18	22.6	23.5	33.9	24.1	31.9	35.0	41.9

*Numbers represent percentages of the entire population, based on the U.S. Census Bureau, Census 2000 Summary File 1. Table based on the following source: Clauss-Ehlers, C.S. (2003). Promoting ecologic health resilience for minority youth: Enhancing health care access through the school health center. *Psychology in the Schools, 40*(3), 265-278. Table reprinted with permission.

DISCUSSION POINTS

The purpose of this discussion is to compare your responses to the questions in the *Steps to Implementation* section with the realities presented in Table 1.2. Discuss the following in your small group:

1. How does the data presented in Table 1.2 compare with your responses to the questions in the *Steps to Implementation* section?
2. What is your reaction to the discrepancy (or similarity) between the data presented in Table 1.2 and your initial response?

Your discussion will depend in part on the different countries and communities in which your course is taught. For those who live in the United States, here are some additional facts to consider:

- Children of color are the fastest growing population in the United States (U.S. Bureau of Census, 1996).
- In 2000, children of color comprised 30% of the entire population (U.S. Bureau of Census, 2000).
- An estimated 3,000 immigrants arrive to the United States each day (Martin & Midgeley, 1994).
- Approximately 1 million immigrants come to the United States each year (Martin & Midgeley, 1994).

DIVERSITY TRAINING ACTIVITY 1.2
SETTING CLASSROOM GROUND RULES

RATIONALE

Notice the range of reactions as the realities of diversity in educational systems are discussed. Some will share their surprise while others will feel the information doesn't pertain to them. It is important to hear all these views without being defensive. After all, the course is about diversity in the current classroom as well as in the surrounding community. It is important to remember that it is only the first day of class. For instructors, the more you can balance the range of viewpoints presented in class, the greater the likelihood that students will work through their assumptions. Setting ground rules will help further this process.

STEPS TO IMPLEMENTATION

1. Your instructor will begin this activity by providing a sample ground rule for the class. Students then follow by contributing their own ground rules.
2. Write ground rules on a flip chart that can be brought to each class.
3. Put an asterisk next to a ground rule each time it is repeated, highlighting the importance of that particular rule for the class.
4. You can refer back to the ground rules when they are broken or are in question.
5. Remember that the class creates the ground rules to reflect participant beliefs and core values--ground rules are not superimposed by the instructor.

DISCUSSION POINTS

The ground rules are a contract that the class has created together, to be applied for the duration of the course. It is important to acknowledge that some topics are controversial or taboo. The contract promotes discussion as it is based on the value of mutual respect. See Table 1.3 for a sample Ground Rules Contract.

Table 1.3 Ground Rules Contract

Only one person talks at a time.
Agree to disagree.
Listen to the other person's viewpoint.
Confidentiality is key—what's discussed in class stays in class.
Talk with one another respectfully.
Arrive on time so that no one is interrupted.
Put chairs in a circle to facilitate classroom discussion.

DIVERSITY TRAINING ACTIVITY 1.3
BEST AND WORST LEARNING EXPERIENCES

RATIONALE

What makes a learning experience memorable? What ingredients facilitate a student's capacity to learn—that make her walk away from a class and remember it for years to come? *Diversity Training Activity 1.3* reviews best and worst learning experiences to identify what creates a positive learning environment. Because you will learn from your peers, the activity also highlights how each student positively contributes to the life of the class. Table 1.4 on page 10 provides examples of student's best and worst learning experiences.

STEPS TO IMPLEMENTATION

1. Share your best and worst learning experiences with the class.
2. Your instructor will create two columns on the board, one entitled Best Learning Experiences and the other called Worst Learning Experiences.
3. Your instructor will write down student responses for each of these categories.

Table 1.4 Best and Worst Learning Experiences

Best Learning Experiences

- Material was relevant to what was going on in my life
- The teacher encouraged, motivated, and inspired me
- The instructor used real life examples and stories from her own work to illustrate the issues
- The class generated an interest in the subject that I never had before
- The classroom had a good structure with a variety of activities
- I felt comfortable sharing
- It was fun, dynamic
- The teacher cared about student success and provided support
- I felt respected, like I could participate

Worst Learning Experiences

- The class was boring, just something to go to
- The instructor favored certain students
- The teacher talked the whole time, we never got to contribute
- Guidelines and requirements for the class were unclear
- The classroom was split into abilities, those put in the lower group lost their motivation
- It felt like the material was dated, the same old thing
- I never got to interact with my peers
- I didn't feel valued or respected
- I couldn't hear the teacher
- I had special educational needs that weren't met
- I was afraid that I would be targeted by my peers

DISCUSSION POINTS

Your discussion will focus on the themes that come up as you discuss what helped you be a good learner and what interfered with academic success. Consider the following:

1. What made you want to learn?
2. What made it difficult to learn?
3. What were the teachers like in your best learning experiences?
4. What were the teachers like in your worst learning experiences?
5. How will you promote a positive learning environment for your students?

Not only does this exercise promote insight regarding your previous classroom experience, it also lets the class decide, discuss, and process how to go about building community in your current classroom as you go through this text.

NOTEBOOK SECTION FOR CHAPTER 1
INTRODUCTION: HOW TO USE THIS MANUAL

A notebook section will be provided at the end of each chapter. The notebook section is to be used for note taking and overall organization of the material presented. Each notebook section will be divided into three parts: Concepts/Theories; Classroom Objectives; and Best Practices. The Concepts/Theories section is for notes about key constructs and ideas presented in class. The Classroom Objectives section is for notes on the goals associated with each topic. The Best Practices section is for notes about strategies to implement that will help you achieve the objectives associated with each topic.

I. CONCEPTS/THEORIES

_____

_____

_____

_____

_____

_____

_____

_____

_____

_____

_____

_____

_____

_____

_____

_____

II. CLASSROOM OBJECTIVES

_____

_____

_____

_____

_____

_____

_____

_____

_____

_____

_____

_____

_____

_____

_____

_____

_____

_____

_____

_____

_____

_____

_____

_____

_____

_____

_____

_____

_____

_____

III. BEST PRACTICES (HOW TO IMPLEMENT THOSE OBJECTIVES IN THE CLASSROOM)

WEB RESOURCES

- The National Association of School Psychologists (NASP) has a section on their Website about culturally competent practice. Information includes definitions of culture and cultural competence, providing culturally competent services, and resources for families. The link is:
  http://www.nasponline.org/culturalcompetence/
- NASP has an article on multicultural and cross-cultural consultation in schools. See the link:
  http://www.nasponline.org/publications/sprsum293.htm

REFERENCES

Clauss-Ehlers, C.S. (2003). Promoting ecologic health resilience for minority youth: Enhancing health care access through the school health center. *Psychology in the Schools, 40*(3), 265-278.

Clauss-Ehlers, C.S., & Weist, M.D. (Eds.). (2004). *Community planning to foster resilience in children.* New York, NY: Kluwer Academic Publishers.

Martin, P., & Midgeley, E. (1994). Immigrants to the United States: Journey to an uncertain destination. *Population Bulletin, 49*(2), 1-47.

Sue, S. (1998). In search of cultural competence in psychotherapy and counseling. *American Psychologist, 53,* 440-448.

U.S. Bureau of Census. (1996). *Current population reports: Population projections of the United States by age, race, and Hispanic origin, 1995-2050.* pp. 25-1130. Washington, DC: U.S. Government Printing Office.

U.S. Bureau of Census (2000). *Census 2000.* Summary File 1.

Chapter 2

How Do We Understand Difference?

A good place to start thinking about diversity is to consider how we understand difference. As defined in *The Random House College Dictionary* (1982), to be different means "1. differing in character or quality; not alike; dissimilar. 2. not identical, separate, or distinct. 3. various, several. 4. unusual, not ordinary." All these definitions point to an underlying theme--difference means more than one. To not be identical, you must have at least two different entities. Understanding difference means you are able to grasp this reality. While this notion seems simple, the opposite is actually the case. People struggle with difference. They gravitate to people who are like them. Was everyone in your high school just like you? Who do you spend time with now? Are your friends like you? Is your partner like you? In what ways?

Chapter 2 is designed to help you examine the notion of the two, three, four, or more unique entities that make up difference. The purpose of the following activities is twofold: 1) to help you understand the complexity associated with difference; and 2) to promote an understanding of difference across a multitude of dimensions.

DIVERSITY TRAINING ACTIVITY 2.1

FIRST IMPRESSION VS. AUTHENTIC IMPRESSION

RATIONALE

One way to break out of the "everyone is the same" mold is to explore how we instinctively develop first impressions based on perceptions. These perceptions may not actually be true, and yet the perceiver may act on them as though they are grounded in reality. The task of this *Diversity Training Activity* is to initiate a dialogue about the concept of difference, its meaning, influence, and how it plays out in life. The Herman Grid exercise highlights the fact that first impressions are not always the right impressions.

STEPS TO IMPLEMENTATION

1. Examine the Herman Grid in Table 2.1.

Table 2.1 The Herman Grid

Source: http://www.nwlink.com/~donclark/leader/diverse2.html
Reproduced with permission.

2. Divide into groups of 5 to 6 students and share your perceptions:

    a) Do you see gray dots at the white intersections on the grid?
    b) Do you believe the gray dots exist?

DISCUSSION POINTS

The Herman Grid is an example of how we see, perceive, believe, and act on things that may not actually exist. When you stare at the black squares on the Herman Grid you will see gray dots at the intersection of the vertical and horizontal white lines. While the gray dots are not really there, seeing them makes the grid look different. Consider the discussion questions below as your group talks about perception, reality, and difference:

1. Have you ever had a mistaken first impression of someone?
2. Has anyone ever had a mistaken first impression of you?
3. What does the Herman Grid suggest about first impressions?
4. What does the Herman Grid suggest about perceptions?
5. What does the Herman Grid suggest about authenticity?
6. What are the implications about the meaning of difference?

DIVERSITY TRAINING ACTIVITY 2.2
MICROCULTURAL IDENTITIES

RATIONALE

Diversity Training Activity 2.2 further explores the numerous variables associated with difference. Subcultures exist in the United States within the context of a larger, overarching macroculture. Gollnick and Chinn (2002) refer to these subcultures as microcultures that they define as "cultural groups...that have distinctive cultural patterns but share some cultural patterns with all members of the U.S macroculture" (p. 18). Those who belong to the same microculture "share traits and values that bind them together as a group" (Gollnick & Chinn, 2002, p. 18).

Being from a shared microculture, however, does not automatically imply sameness. Two women can share the same gender, for instance, and be very different in terms of how they view their role as women. Two individuals can be immigrants and yet have very different experiences. One person has family ties and fluency in the new language while the other immigrated without family connections or fluency.

The individual's identification with microcultural groups is determined by social and historical influences as well as membership in other microcultures. In the previous example, the intersection of language and immigrant experience play out very differently for each individual. The implication is that the individual with family support and knowledge of the new language will have more resources than the person who lacks these supports.

This suggests that microcultural identities occur on a continuum of sameness and difference. Identity is influenced by both life experience and membership in other subcultures. Not only must we look at the continuum of sameness and difference for each microculture, we must also consider how each microcultural continuum interacts with other microcultures (i.e., in this example immigration and language) and in the dominant culture (i.e., how each individual's microcultural experience interacts with the larger society).

STEPS TO IMPLEMENTATION

1. Your instructor will have each student share a microcultural identity (i.e., race, gender, ethnicity). After sharing the identity, each student is to mention aspects of sameness and difference for the microculture. For instance, aspects of difference for gender can include (but are not limited to) masculine, feminine, and androgynous orientations.
2. Your instructor will list each microcultural identity on the board along with related similarities and differences. You can record them on the figure presented in Table 2.2.

DISCUSSION POINTS

Examine the dimensions of microcultural difference after everyone has made a contribution. A key point for discussion concerns the interaction and overlap of being a member of more than one microculture. Another area for discussion involves whether dimensions of microcultures were omitted and what this means for the class. Specific questions are:

1. What do you make of the vast number of microcultures identified by the class?
2. How does the continuum of sameness and difference within each microculture influence how it is experienced? Were any microcultures

not mentioned that you can think of now? What does it mean that they were left out?

3. What are the connections and interrelationships among the microcultures? Do you associate some microcultures with others more readily? What influences your association?

Table 2.2 Microcultural Identities

Document the microcultural identity along with aspects of sameness and difference in the graph below. Add more segments as each class participant reports a relevant identity.

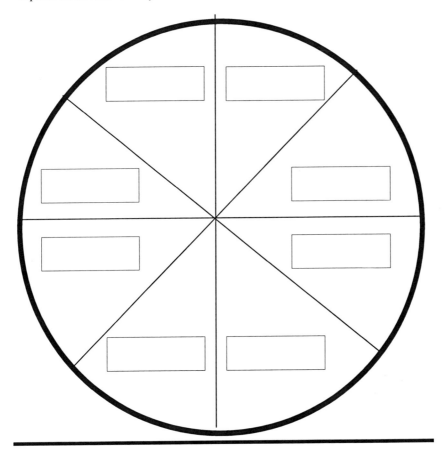

DIVERSITY TRAINING ACTIVITY 2.3

EXPERIENCES OF DIFFERENCE

RATIONALE

The purpose of *Diversity Training Activity 2.3* is to help you delve deeper into the emotional aspect of difference. Perhaps you believe that you do not have an experience of difference and feel this topic does not apply to you. This exercise explores a time when you did feel different, how you felt about it, and how this awareness can help you empathize with differences that others experience. Key themes associated with difference will become apparent as participants share their stories.

STEPS TO IMPLEMENTATION

1. Your instructor will go around the room and have each student recall a time he felt different. You might remember being the only student in class who wore glasses or had a short haircut. The magnitude of the difference is not important--how you felt about the difference you experienced is what matters in this exercise.
2. When you talk about your experience, share the feelings that came up for you during this time.
3. As you listen to the experiences presented, identify the common themes associated with difference. The questions below will guide you in your efforts.

DISCUSSION POINTS

1. What did you notice about yours and other people's reactions to experiences of difference? What feelings emerged for people as they talked about a time they felt different? What common themes came out of your discussion?
2. What do these feelings suggest about how difference is generally viewed?
3. How can we begin to unlearn some of the negative assumptions we have about difference?

NOTEBOOK SECTION FOR CHAPTER 2

HOW DO WE UNDERSTAND DIFFERENCE?

I. CONCEPTS/THEORIES

_____

_____

_____

_____

_____

_____

_____

_____

_____

_____

_____

_____

_____

_____

_____

_____

_____

_____

_____

_____

_____

_____

_____

_____

_____

_____

_____

_____

_____

II. CLASSROOM OBJECTIVES

_____

_____

_____

_____

_____

_____

_____

_____

_____

_____

_____

_____

_____

_____

_____

_____

_____

_____

_____

_____

_____

_____

_____

_____

_____

_____

_____

III. BEST PRACTICES (HOW TO IMPLEMENT THOSE OBJECTIVES IN THE CLASSROOM)

WEB RESOURCES

- The YouthNOISE Website includes information on tolerance and understanding difference. Topics include "What Did You Do With the Hate?" and "Islams, Muslims, Arabs, and Intolerance." The link is: http://www.youthnoise.com/home/
- The Center for Instructional Development and Research at the University of Washington has a Web page devoted to the perspectives, strategies, and resources of inclusive teaching. Key topics for understanding difference are equitable class participation, perspectives on what excludes students, support for student success, and planning for diversity in teaching. The link is: http://depts.washington.edu/cidrweb/inclusive/

REFERENCES

Diversity activities and ice-breakers. (n.d.). Retrieved October 2, 2004, from http://www.nwlink.com/~donclark/leader/diverse2.html

Gollnick, D.M., & Chinn, P.C. (2002). *Multicultural education in a pluralistic society* (6th Edition). Upper Saddle River, NJ: Merrill Prentice Hall.

Stein, J. (1982). *The Random House college dictionary: Revised edition.* New York, NY: Random House.

Section 2

Dimensions of Difference: Culture, Socioeconomic Status, Race, Ethnicity, Language, and Parental Partnership

Chapter 3
Cultural Values and Worldview

Cultural values characterize how we operate, although often out of our awareness. Cultural values are like the dust that surrounds a light bulb--we are unaware it exists until we turn on the light and see it. Carter and Helms (1990) define cultural value orientations as "dimensions that members of a particular group consider important and desirable...what it values, [what] guides the behavior of its individuals, forms the basis for group norms, and dictates lifestyles that are deemed appropriate for group members" (p. 106).

Worldview refers to individual and societal cultural values. It concerns your value-oriented philosophy about life and general framework for understanding the world. Worldview informs how we understand and act on the information we receive (Carter & Helms, 1990). Culture and worldview are not the same, although they are often used interchangeably. Culture is "broadly defined as a common heritage or set of beliefs, norms and values. It refers to the shared and largely learned, attributes of a group of people" (United States Department of Health and Human Services, 2001, p. 9). This differs from worldview that involves how people perceive their relationship to the world, including their values, beliefs, and assumptions (Sue, 1981).

Worldview also influences how individuals and societal groups value achievements. Western educational systems, for instance, often focus on having students develop their problem solving capabilities--the student must master a problem to be successful and achieve in the classroom. Educational success is tied to the idea that you must compete to be happy in life. A presentation I attended about how to enroll your child in competitive private schools provides a telling example. The speaker shared how many parents truly believe that enrollment in the "right" preschool means their child will get into the "right" elementary school, the "right" high school, and the perfect college, all of which will ultimately translate into a happy, productive life. This competitive striving puts a lot of pressure on the child, not to mention the parent.

You the educator will be more effective if the child's social philosophies, language, values, and the importance of family relationships are understood. It is critical to understand children and parents in the context of their respective worldviews. Sensitivity to the worldview of others also requires an awareness of your worldview and cultural values. Breakdowns in communication and collaboration occur when cultural value systems are enforced on others. The following *Diversity Training Activities* are geared to make you aware of how worldviews influence our lives.

DIVERSITY TRAINING ACTIVITY 3.1
CULTURAL VALUES AWARENESS

RATIONALE

Kluckhohn and Strodtbeck (1961) developed a theory of variation in value orientations. These anthropologists traveled throughout the world to determine the common problems and solutions faced by all societies. Their theory determined that "a) value orientations represent a limited number of common human problems; b) the need to find solutions to these common human problems are shared by all cultures; and c) cultures are limited in the number and variety of solutions that are possible" (Carter & Helms, 1990, p. 106). Kluckhohn and Strodtbeck (1961) found that societies around the world share five common human aspects of life, each having one of three possible solutions. *Diversity Training Activity 3.1* spells out their theory of cultural values and encourages you to consider how it influences your day-to-day interactions.

STEPS TO IMPLEMENTATION

1. Kluckhohn and Strodtbeck's (1961) main question was: What do you think are the five common human problems faced by societies throughout the world? Write your response to this question below.

_____

_____

_____

_____

_____

Kluckhohn and Strodtbeck (1961) identified five common human problems faced by societies: Human Nature; Person-Nature; Time; Activity; and Social Relations (See Table 3.1 for a visual representation of Kluckhohn and Strodtbeck's theory).

Table 3.1 Kluckhohn and Strodtbeck's (1961) Theory of Worldview and Cultural Values

COMMON HUMAN PROBLEM	POSSIBLE RESOLUTION	POSSIBLE RESOLUTION	POSSIBLE RESOLUTION
Human Nature	Evil	Mixed	Good
Person-Nature	Subjugation	Mastery	Harmony
Time	Past	Future	Present
Activity	Being	Doing	Being-in-Becoming
Social Relations	Collateral	Individual	Lineal

Human Nature. This common aspect of life refers to how societies view the innate nature of individuals. The three solutions to the problem of Human Nature are evil, mixed, and good. If the societal view is that human nature is evil, the thought is that people are basically born with a sense of evil and will treat others badly. A mixed view of human nature means that people are both good and evil. A good view of human nature reflects the belief that people and societies are basically good and well-intentioned. Kluckhohn and Strodtbeck (1961) believed that societal views of human nature shape how a culture deals with its people. For instance, a society that believes people are basically evil will develop laws to protect citizens from the evil part of one another.

Person-Nature. This common human problem refers to how societies position themselves in terms of their relationship to their natural surroundings. The three resolutions to Person-Nature are subjugation to nature, harmony with nature, and mastery of nature. Subjugation to nature is the belief that natural surroundings are in control, not human beings. Societies who believe in subjugation to nature, for instance, view destruction by a hurricane as nature's will.

Harmony with nature refers to those societies that value living alongside natural surroundings rather than controlling or being controlled by them. Japan's concept of Morita therapy is an example of harmony with nature as negative emotions are to be accepted rather than changed. From this perspective, mental health intervention works to address how all emotions are a part of life--the mastery or change of such feelings are not a focus of treatment.

Mastery of nature means the desire to control nature. Societies that value mastery of nature, for instance, view hurricanes as phenomena that must be conquered, predicted, and controlled. Societies with this value consider mental health intervention as a way to change problems presented by patients in a therapeutic setting.

Time. This common human problem reflects the society's temporal focus. The three possible resolutions to Time are past, present, and future. Cultures with a past temporal focus consider history of experience, past customs, and the value of ancestors. Societies that value the present are focused on the here-and-now rather than the past or the future. Future-focused societies plan for upcoming events and prepare for what they believe the future holds.

Activity. Activity refers to how human beings and their respective societies conduct day-to-day actions and behaviors. The three resolutions to Activity are being, being-in-becoming, and doing. Being refers to activity that is guided by spontaneity. The ability to express the desires and emotions of the moment are valued. Being-in-becoming concerns activities that are reflective and thoughtful. The doing resolution values actions that demonstrate accomplishment. Societies that prescribe to the doing resolution value the end result and ability to produce.

Social Relations. This common human problem refers to how societies conduct their interpersonal relationships. The three resolutions for Social Relations are collateral, individual, and lineal. Collateral relationships refer to those societies that value the group more than the individual. Individual needs come second to those of the group or family. In contrast, societies that value individual relationships prioritize the individual's unique needs and desires. Societies characterized by lineal relationships are those with clear, established hierarchies that structure and organize social relationships.

DISCUSSION POINTS

The Kluckhohn and Strodtbeck (1961) cultural values orientations model provides a framework for understanding how people resolve common human problems through different lenses. How societies respond to these five global problems shapes their perceptions, what they value, and how they operate. The questions below form the focus of class discussion about cultural values and worldview. Discuss the following with the entire class:

1. Examine Table 3.1 on page 31 and identify the resolutions that reflect how you respond to the five common human problems. Circle each.
2. What influenced your cultural values?
3. Now circle the resolutions that characterize mainstream societal values.

4. What differences exist between your cultural values and those that characterize your society?
5. How do you negotiate these differences in everyday interactions?
6. What implications does the cultural values orientation model have for educational practice in a diverse classroom?

DIVERSITY TRAINING ACTIVITY 3.2
U.S. VALUES ACTIVITY WORKSHEET

RATIONALE

Diversity Training Activity 3.2 promotes additional understanding about dominant cultural values in the United States.

STEPS TO IMPLEMENTATION

1. The qualities below reflect differing societal values. Circle the response from each list that you think best represents dominant U.S. cultural values.
2. Remember that circling a word or phrase does not mean you subscribe to that value. It means you see the phrase as accurately describing mainstream cultural values.

LIST A	LIST B
1. Time and its control	Human interaction
2. Cooperation	Competition
3. Past orientation	Future orientation
4. Equality/Fairness	Hierarchy/Rank/Status
5. Self-help/Initiative	Birthright/Inheritance
6. Fate/Destiny	Control of nature
7. "Being" orientation	"Doing" orientation
8. Progress	Tradition
9. Formality	Informality
10. Directness/Openness/Honesty	Indirectness/Ritual/"Face"
11. Materialism/Acquisitiveness	Spiritualism/Detachment
12. Idealism/Theory	Practicality/Efficiency
13. Group's welfare/Dependence	Individualism/Independence

From Kohls, L.R. (n.d.). *The values Americans live by.* Retrieved June 2, 2005, from http://omni.cc.purdue.edu/~corax/kohlsamericanvalues.html Reprinted with permission.

DISCUSSION POINTS

Key points for discussion concern the implications of these cultural value choices on educational outcomes. Specific questions are:

1. How do dominant U.S. cultural values play out in the U.S. educational system?
2. What implications do these values have for educational systems?
3. What implications do these values have for educators?
4. How will you work with a child in an educational setting whose cultural values differ from your own?

DIVERSITY TRAINING ACTIVITY 3.3

PROFESSIONAL CULTURAL BIASES IN EDUCATION

RATIONALE

Diversity Training Activity 3.3 relates your knowledge of cultural values to the educational setting. Table 3.2 shows how ignoring cultural values is detrimental to the diverse classroom learner.

Table 3.2 Professional Cultural Biases in Education

HUMAN PROBLEM	PROFESSIONAL CULTURAL VALUES	PROBLEMS FOR OTHER CULTURES
SOCIAL RELATIONS	Individualism, independence, and autonomy are highly valued in the classroom.	Students who value the group may be poor performers in a competitive environment.
ACTIVITY	Action and doing. The student must always do something about a situation.	Exploration, understanding, and acceptance may be more important than a final product.
TIME	Rigid time schedule. Time is seen as a commodity.	Rigid time constraints do not meet the needs of all students. Children with special needs who need more time to take exams are one such example.
COMMUNICATION	Student ability is assessed by the extent to which the student is verbal, makes direct eye contact, and speaks standard English. These are markers for educational success.	Nonverbal communication is critical for context-oriented cultures. Nonverbal behaviors have different meanings for different racial/cultural groups. Students who don't speak English may be misjudged as lacking intelligence.

STEPS TO IMPLEMENTATION

1. Your instructor will lead the discussion about this activity with the class as a whole.
2. Examine Table 3.2 and consider the contrast between professional cultural values and the problems they raise for other cultures.

DISCUSSION POINTS

Questions for discussion are:

1. What was your reaction to differences between professional cultural values and problems for other cultures?
2. How do you expect to see these difficulties as a teacher in the school system?
3. How will you address some of these biases in your own teaching practice?
4. Given the information presented in this chapter, what specifically do you want to change about your approach to teaching?
5. How will you go about implementing these changes?

These questions provide a starting point for discussion. The themes raised here will be revisited as you explore aspects of diversity throughout the text.

NOTEBOOK SECTION FOR CHAPTER 3
CULTURAL VALUES AND WORLDVIEW

I. CONCEPTS/THEORIES

_____

_____

_____

_____

_____

_____

_____

_____

_____

_____

_____

_____

_____

_____

_____

_____

_____

_____

_____

_____

_____

_____

_____

_____

_____

II. CLASSROOM OBJECTIVES

III. BEST PRACTICES (HOW TO IMPLEMENT THOSE OBJECTIVES IN THE CLASSROOM)

WEB RESOURCES

- The University of Colorado has information on instructive approaches to conflict. One area focuses on communication tools for understanding difference. Cultural value orientations like high-context vs. low-context communication and individual vs. communitarian concepts of self and other are discussed. The link is:
  http://www.intractableconflict.org/m/communication_tools.jsp

REFERENCES

Carter, R.T., & Helms, J.E. (1990). White attitudes and cultural values. In J.E. Helms (Ed.), *Black and white racial identity: Theory, research, and practice* (pp. 104-118). New York, NY: Greenwood Press.

Kluckhohn, F.R., & Strodtbeck, F.L. (1961). *Variations in value orientations.* Evanston, IL: Row Paterson.

Kohls, L.R. (n.d.). The values Americans live by. Retrieved June 2, 2005, from http://omni.cc.purdue.edu/~corax/kohlsamericanvalues.html

Sue, D.W. (1981). *Counseling the culturally different: Theory and practice.* New York, NY: John Wiley & Sons.

U.S. Department of Health and Human Services (2001). *Mental health: Culture, race, and ethnicity—A supplement to Mental health: A report of the Surgeon General.* Rockville, MD: U.S. Department of Health and Human Services, Public Health Service, Office of the Surgeon General.

Chapter 4

Socioeconomic Status

Socio-economic status (SES) refers to a position on an economic hierarchy based upon income, education, and occupation. SES influences one's lifestyle, prestige, power, and control of resources (Berk, 2002; Liu et al, 2004). The U.S. Bureau of the Census (2003) bases SES on income, occupation, and educational attainment. Scholars often stratify social class using the categories of lower class, working class, middle class, upper middle class, and upper class. While beyond the scope of this chapter, readers are encouraged to consult Wikipedia (2004) for a complete description of social class terms. This chapter will focus on the idea of social mobility as a U.S. myth and implications for educational systems.

Educational Initiatives and Implications for Educators

SES implies mobility to different economic levels, yet many scholars have posited that social mobility is a U.S. myth (Liu et al., 2004). The belief that hard work and perseverance is all you need to "make it" is refuted by the reality that many people don't have access to resources. The idea that people are able to "pull themselves up by their bootstraps" leads to blaming the poor for their situation. The reality is that limited opportunities, differential pay for men and women, and inadequate educational resources make upward mobility quite difficult, if not impossible.

According to Banks and McGee Banks (2004), the structure of schooling, social beliefs, and curricular practices influence educational inequalities. One study found that teachers have lower expectations for poor children in comparison to their middle class counterparts. This finding remained constant even when both groups of children had similar IQ scores and achievements (Banks & McGee Banks, 2004).

Public schools in the U.S. are often organized by local districts that are identified as having either high or low incomes. Designations are determined by the wealth of the individuals living in the district and the property value of their homes. Low-income districts often have limited access to qualified teachers, books, computers, and other supplies as they are partially funded by district taxes. If residents make less money, they have less taxable income. This means less funding for the school. The result is extreme disparity between school districts, some of which are located right next to each other. Several controversial educational initiatives address the issue of inequality among students from neighborhoods with different resources. School choice, charter schools, magnet schools, and assessment reform are four initiatives discussed below.

School choice. School choice is an educational reform that lets parents decide what school they want their children to attend. School choice gives families and students the opportunity to select publicly funded alternatives to traditional neighborhood schools. Those who support school choice say that this system lets students from low SES backgrounds have equal access to better education.

Charter schools. Charter schools also aim to decrease educational inequities among students. Charter school legislation was first passed in the 1990s and resulted in the development of approximately 3,000 new schools (U.S. Charter Schools, n.d.). Charter schools were developed to break free of traditional public school regulations by offering a publicly funded alternative. Differences between charter schools and public schools include different curriculums, teaching styles, and methods of assessment. Charter schools are independent of the public school system and design their programs to meet the specific needs of their surrounding communities (U.S. Charter Schools, n.d.).

Magnet schools. Magnet schools are publicly funded schools that specialize in content areas like academics, science, the fine arts, performing arts, and the humanities. Magnet schools draw students from the surrounding geographical region, a policy initiated to combat and put an end to racial segregation. There are magnet schools for elementary, middle school, and high school students. Some involve a competitive entrance process while others use a lottery system. Magnet schools are often criticized for only educating gifted and talented students. Research indicates, however, that small class size and good instructional style are what promotes good academic standing (Doyle & Levine, 1984).

Assessment reform. Assessment reform also works to diminish social inequities among students. While some believe that implementing more standardized tests at various grade levels will promote accountability for teachers and schools, others seek to eliminate standardization in favor of authentic assessments. Proponents of this view want children to show what they have learned in real-life practical ways.

Professional development is needed, however, if assessment reform is to occur. Teachers must learn how to use new assessment techniques to move away from the traditional standardized methods that they know. Training can help teachers take a broad approach to the acquisition of knowledge and teach them how to use assessment tools like short-answer questions, open-ended questions, interviews, performance events, performance tasks, portfolios, observations, and anecdotal documentation. Assessment reform should also occur at local, state, and national levels so that student performance is measured in a comprehensive manner (Roeber, 1995).

The following *Diversity Training Activities* explore the concept of socioeconomic status and its interface with the school system.

DIVERSITY TRAINING ACTIVITY 4.1
EDUCATIONAL INITIATIVES

RATIONALE

Controversial educational initiatives such as school choice, charter schools, magnet schools, and assessment reform are supported by the desire to equalize education for students. *Diveristy Training Activity 4.1, Educational Initiatives,* encourages you to consider the various perspectives associated with these issues.

STEPS TO IMPLEMENTATION

1. Your instructor will organize the class into small groups of 5 to 6 students.
2. Each group will select one initiative (i.e., school choice, charter schools, magnet schools, or assessment reform) and discuss its advantages and disadvantages.

DISCUSSION POINTS

Discussion for this *Diveristy Training Activity* revolves around how educational policy and practice interact with socioeconomic status. Questions for discussion include:

1. What was your reaction to the advantages and disadvantages associated with the educational initiative discussed in your group?
2. How did your own SES influence your evaluation of the advantages and disadvantages associated with the initiative?
3. How will these differences play out for teachers in the school system?
4. Should this initiative be implemented in your area?
5. How will you work with parents involved in the initiative?

DIVERSITY TRAINING ACTIVITY 4.2

VIDEO SNAPSHOT:
PEOPLE LIKE US: SOCIAL CLASS IN AMERICA (ALVAREZ & KOLKER, 2001)

RATIONALE

The documentary *People Like Us: Social class in America* examines class structure in the United States (Alvarez & Kolker, 2001). The purpose of the film is to have people learn about how social class works in the United States.

STEPS TO IMPLEMENTATION

1. Your instructor will obtain the movie from the library or a video store or purchase it from the PBS website (http://www.pbs.org/peoplelikeus).
2. Watch the different stories that comprise the film.
3. Discuss your thoughts about the movie with the class.

DISCUSSION POINTS

Discussion points for *People Like Us* help students examine the realities of socioeconomic status. Questions for discussion include:

1. What was your reaction to the film?
2. What has the film taught you about the influence of social class in educational settings?
3. What implications does the film have for your role as an educator?

NOTEBOOK SECTION FOR CHAPTER 4
SOCIOECONOMIC STATUS

I. CONCEPTS/THEORIES

II. CLASSROOM OBJECTIVES

III. BEST PRACTICES (HOW TO IMPLEMENT THOSE OBJECTIVES IN THE CLASSROOM)

WEB RESOURCES

- *People Like Us: Social class in America* (Alvarez & Kolker, 2001) is a PBS documentary that examines class structure in the United States by illustrating the lives of people from different social class backgrounds. The link below is a direct connection to the People Like Us Website that is a companion to the film. The Website provides games, stories, resources, and classroom lessons geared to enhance knowledge about social class distinctions. The link is:
  http://www.pbs.org/peoplelikeus/about/top.html
- The National Center for Children in Poverty is a research and policy organization at Columbia University's Mailman School of Public Health. The Website offers a wide range of information that includes demographic data about children who live in low-income families, child poverty and low-income rates by state, family poverty and low-income rates by states, and fact sheets on topics such as child support and parent employment in low-income families. The link is:
  http://www.nccp.org/cat_8.html

REFERENCES

Alvarez, L. (Producer & Director), & Kolker, A. (Producer & Director). (2001). *People like us: Social class in America* [Documentary special for public television]. Washington D.C.: Public Broadcasting Service.

Banks, J.A., & McGee Banks, C.A. (2004) *Multicultural education: Issues and perspectives.* Hoboken, NJ: John Wiley & Sons, Inc.

Battin-Pearson, S., Abbot, R.D., Hill, K.G., Catalano, R.F., Hawkins, J.D., & Newcomb, M.D. (2000). Predictors of early high school dropout: A test of five theories. *Journal of Educational Psychology, 92*(3), 568-582.

Begoray, D., & Slovinksy, K. (1997). Pearls in shells: Preparing teachers to accommodate gifted low income populations. *Roeper Review, 20*(1), 45-50.

Coolahan, K., Fantuzzo, J., Mendez, J., & McDermott, P. (2000). Preschool peer interactions and readiness to learn: Relationships between classroom peer play and learning behaviors and conduct. *Journal of Educational Psychology, 92*(3), 458-465.

Doyle, D.P., & Levine, M. (1984). Magnet schools: Choice and quality in public education. *Phi Delta Kappan, 66,* 265-270.

Liu, W.M., Ali, S.R., Soleck, G., Hopps, J., Dunston, K., & Pickett, T. (2004). Using social class in counseling psychology research. *Journal of Counseling Psychology, 51*(1), 3-18.

Lu, H.H., & Koball, H. (2003). *The changing demographics of low-income families and their children.* Retrieved December 15, 2004, from http://www.nccp.org/media/lat03b-text.pdf

National Center for Children in Poverty. (2004). *Demographics.* Retrieved December 15, 2004, from http://www.nccp.org/cat_8.html

Renchler, R. (1993). *Poverty and learning.* Eugene, OR: ERIC Clearinghouse on Educational Management (ERIC Document Reproduction Service No. ED357433). Retrieved June 14, 2005, from http://www.ericdigests.org/1993/poverty.htm

Roeber, E. (1995). *Emerging student assessment systems for school reform*. Greensboro, NC: Eric Clearinghouse on Counseling and Student Services (ERIC Document Reproduction Service No. ED 389959). Retrieved June 12, 2005, from http://www.ericdigests.org/1996-3/reform.htm

U.S. Bureau of the Census. (2003). *Poverty: 2003 highlights*. Retrieved December 9, 2004, from http://www.census.gov/hhes/poverty/poverty03/pov03hi.html

U.S. Charter Schools (n.d.). *U.S. charter schools*. Retrieved June 11, 2005, from http://www.uscharterschools.org/lpt/uscs_docs/329

Wikipedia (2004). *Social structure of the United States*. Retrieved December 17, 2004, from http://en.wikipedia.org/wiki/Social_structure_of_the_United_States

Chapter 5
Race and Ethnicity

The terms culture, race and ethnicity are often mistakenly used interchangeably. The terms actually have different meanings and represent different concepts. Chapter 5 clarifies the concepts of race and ethnicity through conceptual definitions and activities.

Race. While race as a biological variable has largely been refuted, the concept of race has social meaning. Societies like the U.S. classify people into social groups based on characteristics that have social significance (U.S. Department of Health and Human Services, 2001). Carter (1995) defines race as a concept that "refers to a *presumed* classification of all human groups on the basis of *visible physical traits or phenotype and behavioral differences.* Inherent in classifying groups in this way is also the presumption of rank order where one group, typically Whites...is the standard by which all others are judged and ranked" (p.15). When race is used as a classification system in North America, assumptions are made about "emotional, cognitive, psychological, intellectual, and moral qualities" based upon physical characteristics (Carter, 1995, p.15). Racism occurs when there is an assumption of the superiority of one race over other races.

Ethnicity. Ethnicity is a cultural heritage that encompasses language, history, and rituals that are passed from one generation to the next. Ethnicity refers to a shared national or religious identity. Someone may describe themselves as Irish, for instance, because they come from Ireland. National or religious origin is the defining factor for ethnicity (U.S. Department of Health and Human Services, 2001).

Prejudice vs. Racism

In its most literal form the term prejudice means to prejudge. We judge people based on previous experience, learned stereotypes, and internalized belief systems. The 16-year-old student who wears baggy jeans and a torn sweatshirt the first day of class is one such example. The educator may assume this student is uninterested in learning because of his sloppy appearance. It turns out, however, that this student is very committed to his education but cannot afford to buy new clothes. The educator's prejudgment has mistakenly put the student in the "disinterested learner" category.

Racism is often equated with prejudice (Carter, 1995). This is problematic because it locates racism in the individual only and ignores larger contextual issues (Carter, 1995). Jones (1981) purports a broader view of racism that encompasses individual, institutional, and cultural factors. Individual racism refers to attitudes, behaviors, and socialization experiences that maintain a belief in White superiority and involve what someone does to someone else on an individual basis (Jones, 1981). Institutional racism concerns institutions that limit the resources, choices, and mobility of different groups of individuals on a racial basis (Jones, 1981). Here the institution (not the individual) systematically denies people from particular racial groups equal access to resources. Institutions may not intend to engage in institutional racism, but organizational structure and policies lead to this outcome. Institutional racism can be seen in housing, education, labor, health, economics, and other quality of life variables.

Cultural racism is a third dimension of racism where society considers some beliefs to be more important than others (Jones, 1981). Cultural racism can be expressed in aesthetics (i.e., how the culture defines beauty), valuing certain art forms above others (i.e., certain types of music), and favoring particular philosophical orientations. The individual who immigrates to the U.S., absorbs the Western notion of a thin-body ideal, and starts to feel badly about her body image is one example of how cultural racism plays out in eating disorders.

Racial/Ethnic Identity Theories

Racial identity theory refers to the individual's psychological orientation to his or her race (Carter, 1995; Clauss, 1999). Several racial identity theories have been proposed in the literature. This chapter will discuss two models presented by Helms (1990b): White racial identity theory and Black racial identity theory (See Helms (1990b) for an extensive review of the two theories). The theories examine within group differences and propose different statuses that capture where the individual is at in terms of racial identity development.

White racial identity development. Helms' model of White racial identity development states that Whites differ in their psychological orientation to race (Helms, 1990c). "The extent to which one is oriented to or away from norms of entitlement and superiority is the extent to which Whites develop as racial beings. Thus, being aware of the person's racial group is not as important as knowing how that person identifies with the group's values and norms" (Clauss, 1999, p. 38).

Helms' (1990c) six White racial identity statuses are: Contact, Disintegration, Reintegration, Pseudo-Independence, Immersion/ Emersion, and Autonomy. Her two-phase process of White racial identity development involves abandoning racism in the first phase (this occurs during the

Contact, Disintegration, and Reintegration statuses) and defining a positive White identity in the second (this occurs during the Pseudo-Independent, Immersion/Emersion, and Autonomy statuses). Racial identity development is not a linear process as the individual does not necessarily go through each status in an orderly progression. In fact, an individual may remain at one status for many years and show no movement at all.

Individuals in the Contact status of racial identity deny the meaning of racial group membership. Individuals at this stage of racial identity are color blind in the sense that they do not recognize the importance of race (Clauss, 1998). An individual at this status of development might say, for instance, "We're all the same" or "Race doesn't matter."

Individuals enter the Disintegration status when experiences make them realize that race is a salient variable in their lives. Individuals in the Disintegration stage of development feel conflicted about their awareness, however, because it conflicts with earlier beliefs.

Reintegration is the third status and most closely resembles old-fashioned racism. According to Helms (1990c), individuals may actively or passively express the attitudes associated with this status. An active expression involves treating people of color as inferior or "engaging in acts of violence or exclusion to maintain White privilege" (Clauss, 1999, p. 43). A passive expression of Reintegration attitudes involves avoiding racially diverse environments.

Pseudo-Independence is the fourth White racial identity development status. Attitudes at this status indicate a shift towards a positive White racial identity. Here the individual begins to consider the role that Whites play in contributing to racism. Individuals start to have an intellectual appreciation of racial differences at this point in their racial identity development.

Pseudo-Independence is followed by the Immersion/Emersion status. At this stage of development Whites begin to explore themselves as racial beings in a non-defensive way. "This process involves the person's attempts to accept his or her heritage without believing it should oppress other races" (Clauss, 1999, p. 45).

Autonomy is the final status of development. Here individuals have an intellectual and emotional appreciation of racial differences. Individuals at this stage of racial identity development are aware of racism and racial norms. They have a flexible worldview, value difference, and pursue interracial interactions.

Black racial identity development. According to Helms (1986), each Black racial identity status represents a unique worldview that characterizes people's cognitive schema about themselves and their world. The four statuses that make up Black racial identity development are: Preencounter, Encounter, Immersion/Emersion, and Internalization. In Preencounter, the Black person depends upon White society for definitions of self and approval. Helms (1990a) writes: "The general theme of the Preencounter stage is idealization of the dominant traditional White world view and, consequently, denigration of a Black world view" (p. 20).

Individuals enter the Encounter status of Black racial identity development when they become confused or conflicted about the meaning of race. It may be that the Black individual has an experience that underscores the salience of race and what it means to be Black. The realization that one must shift away from the attitudes that characterize the Preencounter status indicates a move towards the Immersion/Emersion status.

The Immersion/Emersion status involves a two-phase process of development. In Immersion, individuals actively explore what it means to be Black. Helms (1990a) writes: "The person psychologically and physically, if possible, withdraws into Blackness and a Black world. He or she thinks, feels, and acts the way he or she believes "authentic" Blacks are supposed to, and judges and evaluates other Blacks on the basis of their conformance to these "idealistic" racial standards" (p. 27). The Emersion aspect of this status occurs when individuals develop a "positive nonstereotypic Afro-American perspective on the world" (Helms, 1990a, p. 28).

Finally, the Internalization status of Black racial identity development refers to the internalization of a positive Black racial identity. Individuals in this status reject racism. They are able to redevelop relationships with White individuals and no longer judge others based on their racial group membership (Helms, 1990a).

Ethnic Identity Development. In addition to models of racial identity development, there are several models of ethnic identity development in the literature (Phinney & Alipuria, 1987). These models address ethnic identity formation or the extent to which individuals understand the implications of their ethnicity and the role it plays in their lives. Phinney and Alipuria (1987) define ethnic identity as "an individual's sense of self as a member of an ethnic group and the attitudes and behaviors associated with that sense" (p. 36).

Phinney (1990) presents a three-stage model of ethnic identity development. In Stage One, Unexamined Ethnic Identity, the individual does not explore his ethnicity. The values of the majority culture are accepted, even when they espouse a negative view of the individual's own ethnic background. The shift from the first to the second stage happens when an event occurs that motivates the individual to search for his ethnic identity. Stage Two, Ethnic Identity Search/Moratorium, involves the process of exploring one's ethnicity. In Stage Three, Ethnic Identity Achievement, the individual has a positive view of his ethnicity. Ethnic background is accepted and a solid ethnic identification is internalized.

The Educator's Role

Your role as a multicultural educator is to be aware of how race and ethnicity play out in the classroom. The three *Diversity Training Activities* below are designed to help you respond fairly to racial/ethnic differences. As with many of the other variables discussed in this text, it is critical that you develop an awareness of yourself as a racial/ethnic being. *Diversity Training Activity 5.1, Video Snapshot: The Color of Fear* (Mun Wah, 1994), is geared to help further that awareness through an in-depth examination of race, ethnicity, and racism. Awareness of one's own biases and assumptions is a key starting point for work as a multicultural educator. Identifying such biases is likely to be a painful process, but one that ultimately helps you transform your classroom approach.

A second component to your role as educator is to be thoughtful and reflective about the nature of activities and instructional materials provided in the classroom. Does the curriculum reflect diverse racial/ethnic experiences? Are books written by authors from different racial/ethnic backgrounds? *Diversity Training Activity 5.2, Integrating a Multiethnic Curriculum,* is designed to help you think about the nature of the curriculum that you develop and implement. Integrating a multiethnic curriculum directly relates to your personal awareness about race and ethnicity. Without the ability to analyze content and materials in terms of these variables, you risk designing a curriculum (and class environment) that is unresponsive to students of color.

A third point concerns how to intervene and respond to racism and discrimination. Hopefully your school has policies in place that address these realities. *Diversity Training Activity 5.3, Student Scenario: Handling Discrimination in the Classroom,* is designed to give you the requisite skills that are needed when racial/ethnic tensions occur in class.

Critical to your role as a multicultural educator is the ability to model proactive, prosocial behavior that sets the tone for the class. Too often my students have shared that they experienced racism in school and no one intervened. This do-nothing course of action sends the message that students aren't valued. It challenges your credibility as a responsive teacher. While *Diversity Training Activity 5.3* presents only one role-play opportunity, you are encouraged to seek out additional training and supervision about how to respond to racism.

DIVERSITY TRAINING ACTIVITY 5.1
VIDEO SNAPSHOT:
THE COLOR OF FEAR (MUN WAH, 1994)

RATIONALE

The Color of Fear (Mun Wah, 1994) presents the experience of eight North American men of Asian, African, Native American, Latino, and European descent. The men meet for a weekend retreat and talk about the realities of racism in their lives. The men discuss the historical basis of oppression and their struggle to be heard. Feelings run their course, starting with anger and frustration and ultimately leading to hope and renewal. The video allows viewers to better understand the complexities associated with race and ethnicity in the United States.

STEPS TO IMPLEMENTATION

1. Your instructor can order the video through the StirFry Seminars & Consulting Website at www.stirfryseminars.com The film is approximately 90 minutes long.
2. After you watch the video, discuss the questions below with your class.

DISCUSSION POINTS

1. What was your overall reaction to the film *The Color of Fear* (Mun Wah, 1994)?
2. What feelings did you experience as you watched the film (remember to stay focused on feelings and not opinions or thoughts)?
3. Who did you identify with the most in the film? Why?
4. Who did you identify with the least in the film? Why?
5. What surprised you the most about the film?
6. What implications does the group session have for educators?
7. How does the film inform your role as a multicultural educator?

DIVERSITY TRAINING ACTIVITY 5.2
INTEGRATING A MULTIETHNIC CURRICULUM

RATIONALE

It is your job to make sure that the course curriculum reflects racial/ethnic diversity. Too often classroom materials and curriculum focus on North American and Western European perspectives. This approach leaves out the diverse perspectives of South America, Central America, Africa, and Asia, among others.

A predominant goal of multicultural education is to provide a curriculum that incorporates diversity in classroom teachings and interactions. This does not mean that one class is offered on the history of Asian Americans or women of color. These add on approaches fail to capture the true value and purpose of a multiethnic curriculum--to incorporate diversity throughout the course. A comprehensive multiethnic curriculum means that you are thoughtful about all aspects of class content: bulletin boards, assignments, guest speakers, books, textbooks, films, written assignments, foods served, field trips, and instructional activities. The purpose of *Diversity Training Activity 5.2* is to learn how to design a class project that reflects the goals of a multiethnic curriculum.

STEPS TO IMPLEMENTATION

1. Table 5.1, Components of a Comprehensive Multiethnic Curriculum, describes how class material can take an inclusive approach.
2. Review Table 5.1 and write a three-page lesson plan that incorporates at least one aspect of the multiethnic curriculum.
3. Your lesson plan should involve an assignment that you want students to complete. It may involve writing a report about a particular book, for instance, or analyzing a historical perspective. Choose any grade level for your plan.
4. Discuss the questions below with your classmates after you complete the assignment.

Table 5.1 Components of a Comprehensive Multiethnic Curriculum

Instructional Resource	Incorporating the Multiethnic Curriculum Approach
Bulletin Boards	Have bulletin boards reflect diverse racial/ethnic groups throughout the year. Students can design the bulletin boards or the instructor can choose a theme that reflects diversity.
Assignments	Coursework and homework should incorporate a range of diverse backgrounds. For instance, a high school social studies lesson can focus on countries other than the United States. Elementary school children can write about cultures other than their own.
Guest Speakers	Guest speakers give students direct contact with diverse experiences. Guest speakers can talk about themes that relate to current course material. Parents can also give presentations about their diverse experiences. Students themselves can be "guest speakers" for the class. Organize an assignment where students give a class presentation focused on the meaning of difference in their lives.
Books and Textbooks	Review the book and textbook selection at the beginning of the school year. Questions to consider are: Whose perspectives are reflected in these books? Are a range of racial/ethnic backgrounds presented? Who are the authors? Do they reflect diverse racial/ethnic backgrounds? Change your reading list based on your responses. From preschool to adult education, many books have been published that represent a range of diverse racial/ethnic perspectives.
Films	The questions presented above also apply to the films you show in class. Do your research and order films that reflect diverse issues and backgrounds.
Written Assignments	What are students being asked to write about? Are they encouraged to consider multiethnic viewpoints? Connect written assignments to class readings. For instance, have students read the book *The House on Mango Street* (Cisneros, 1991) and write about the main character. This assignment creates a synergy between reading and writing in a multiethnic context.
Foods Served	How can foods that reflect different racial/ethnic backgrounds be part of the course curriculum? Students can bring in food to share with their classmates. The school can serve foods that represent different backgrounds.
Field Trips	Field trips can visit destinations that reflect diverse perspectives and worldviews.
Instructional Activities	Students can conduct research on non-Western countries, create oral histories, and organize interview projects that incorporate diverse perspectives.

DISCUSSION POINTS

1. How does the comprehensive multiethnic curriculum approach encourage you to incorporate perspectives you may have previously omitted?
2. What did you learn from writing a lesson plan that incorporates the multiethnic curriculum approach?
3. Is there one particular component of the multiethnic curriculum that you feel particularly comfortable with? Why?
4. Is there one particular component of the multiethnic curriculum that you feel uncomfortable with? Why?
5. How will you get go about getting support for your curriculum?
6. Who will you consult as you develop your multiethnic curriculum?
7. Is there a role for parent involvement? What does that role look like?
8. How can you get students involved?
9. Are there groups and organizations that you can collaborate with as you develop your multiethnic curriculum?
10. What barriers to developing a multiethnic curriculum do you envision?
11. How will you deal with these challenges?
12. What other strategies will you use to implement the multiethnic curriculum approach in your classroom?
13. Will you teach other educators in your school about the approach? If yes, how will you go about doing this?
14. How will you evaluate your curriculum at the end of the year?
15. Whose input will be valuable as you determine what your students have learned about difference?
16. Is there a way to get interest in your curriculum from other schools in your district?
17. How will you go about raising this interest?

DIVERSITY TRAINING ACTIVITY 5.3

STUDENT SCENARIO:
HANDLING DISCRIMINATION IN THE CLASSROOM

RATIONALE

The purpose of *Diversity Training Activity 5.3* is to learn how to manage discrimination in the classroom. It is hoped that the role-play will help you feel better equipped to intervene on behalf of your students when discriminatory behaviors occur.

STEPS TO IMPLEMENTATION

1. Read the scenario below:

    You are a teacher dealing with the aftermath of the terrorist attacks that occurred on September 11th, 2001. Your school is quite diverse and there are several Arab children in your third grade class. Your students are walking in line on their way to an assembly when one student turns to his Arab classmate and shouts, "You terrorist!" You witness this incident and wonder how to respond at that moment.

2. Your instructor will divide the class into groups of 5 to 6 students to discuss how you will handle this situation.

DISCUSSION POINTS

1. What is your initial reaction to the scenario presented above?
2. As the teacher in this situation, how will you respond?
3. What will you say to the student, his parents, and school administrators about the incident?
4. How will you talk with the class about racial/ethnic relations after this incident?

NOTEBOOK SECTION FOR CHAPTER 5
RACE AND ETHNICITY

I. CONCEPTS/THEORIES

II. CLASSROOM OBJECTIVES

_____

_____

_____

_____

_____

_____

_____

_____

_____

_____

_____

_____

_____

_____

_____

_____

_____

_____

_____

_____

_____

_____

_____

_____

_____

_____

III. BEST PRACTICES (HOW TO IMPLEMENT THOSE OBJECTIVES IN THE CLASSROOM)

_____

_____

_____

_____

_____

_____

_____

_____

_____

_____

_____

_____

_____

_____

_____

_____

_____

_____

_____

_____

_____

_____

_____

_____

_____

_____

WEB RESOURCES

- The National Association for the Advancement of Colored People (NAACP) focuses on the civil rights of African Americans and other minorities. The NAACP has an education advocacy agenda that aims to give all students access to a quality education. The NAACP Education Department works to prevent racial discrimination in education, promote educational excellence, and foster equal opportunity. The link for the NAACP Website is:

   http://www.naacp.org/

   The direct link for the NAACP Education Department is:

   http://www.naacp.org/departments/education/education_index.html

- The Southern Poverty Law Center has a Web page entitled Teaching Tolerance that focuses on anti-bias education for K-12 teachers. Teaching tools are presented such as classroom activities and resources organized by grade and subject. Grant opportunities for K-12 teachers who develop anti-bias projects in their schools and communities are also provided. The link on the Southern Poverty Law Center that brings you to their Teaching Tolerance Web page is:

   http://www.splcenter.org/center/tt/teach.jsp

REFERENCES

Carter, R.T. (1995). *The influence of race and racial identity in psychotherapy: Toward a racially inclusive model.* New York: John Wiley & Sons, Inc.

Cisneros, S. (1991). *The house on Mango Street.* New York: Vintage Contemporaries.

Clauss, C. S. (1999). Degrees of distance: The relationship between White racial identity and social distance phenomena in American society (Doctoral dissertation, Teachers College, Columbia University). *Dissertation Abstracts International,* 9916865, 60-01B.

Gollnick, D.M., & Chinn, P.C. (2002*). Multicultural education in a pluralistic society* (6th ed). Upper Saddle River, NJ: Merrill Prentice Hall.

Helms, J.E. (1986). Expanding racial identity theory to cover counseling process. *Journal of Counseling Psychology, 33*(1), 62-64.

Helms, J.E. (1990a). An overview of Black racial identity theory. In J.E. Helms (Ed.), *Black and white racial identity: Theory, research, and practice* (pp. 9-32). New York, NY: Greenwood Press.

Helms, J.E. (1990b). *Black and white racial identity: Theory, research, and practice.* New York, NY: Greenwood Press.

Helms, J.E. (1990c). Toward a model of White racial identity. In J.E. Helms (Ed.), *Black and white racial identity: Theory, research, and practice* (pp. 49-66). New York, NY: Greenwood Press.

Jones, J.M. (1981). The concept of racism and its changing reality. In B.P. Bowser & R.G. Hunt (Eds.), *Impacts of racism on White Americans* (pp. 27-49). Thousand Oaks, CA: Sage Publications.

Lorde, A. (1995). Age, race, class, and sex: Women redefining difference. In J. Arthur & A. Shapiro (Eds.), *Campus wars: Multiculturalism and the politics of difference* (pp. 191-198). Boulder, CO: Westview Press.

Mun Wah, L. (Producer & Director). (1994). *The color of fear*. [Film]. Oakland, CA: StirFry Seminars & Consulting.

Phinney, J.S. (1990). Ethnic identity in adolescents and adults: Review of research. *Psychological Bulletin, 108*(3), 499-514.

Phinney, J.S., & Alipuria, L. (1987). Ethnic identity in older adolescents from four ethnic groups. Paper presented at the Biennial Meeting of the Society for Research in Child Development, Baltimore (ERIC Document Reproduction Service No. Ed 283 058).

U.S. Department of Health and Human Services (2001). *Mental health: Culture, race, and ethnicity—A supplement to Mental health: A report of the Surgeon General*. Rockville, MD: U.S. Department of Health and Human Services, Public Health Service, Office of the Surgeon General.

Chapter 6
Language in the Classroom

Language plays a definite role in the life of the classroom. Educators use language to "create a space to respond, relate, and analyze the verbalizations that the individual reveals" (Clauss, 1998, p. 188). Elements of conversational interaction allow educators to work with and understand their students. Educators bring their own language background and history to the classroom space they share with diverse language learners. As such, there is a cross-cultural context in which communication between students and educators occurs (Dana, 1996; Javier 1995).

While language is often taken for granted, the fact that it is the primary mechanism for learning and communication makes it a critical classroom variable. Educators must be aware of the language systems in which their students experience their world. Thoughtfulness about how language influences children involves examining the language space from which children communicate, how this process informs a sense of self, how children experience themselves when speaking different languages, and how language reflects culture (Clauss, 1998).

Language and culture are entwined as language is representational of the child's cultural context. For instance, the American cultural pattern that values individual accomplishment is reflected in the capitalization of the word *I* (Clauss, 1998). This reality contrasts with the word for *I* in Spanish, *yo*, which is not capitalized and symbolizes the value placed on family.

This cultural expression of language has implications for education. The U.S. educational system values individual competition and accomplishment. We see this in educational practices such as grading based on a curve, individual assignments, and students who study on their own rather than in groups. The individualistic nature of such instruction may feel culturally dystonic for students from group-oriented cultures who expect the class to work together as a team.

Educators are obligated to let each child learn in the language spoken at home until the child can adequately perform in English. This means that the educator is patient with the child and works to find supportive resources while new language systems develop. Too often I have worked with Spanish speaking children whose parents are terrified because the teacher wants to refer them to a special education classroom. These children were not performing poorly because they had a learning disability. Rather, they simply needed time to adjust to the dominant language and cultural nuances presented in the classroom.

One eight-year-old Guatemalan child, for instance, repeatedly lost grade points for not participating in class. The concept of class participation was completely new for a child who was taught to adhere to the value of *respeto*. Respect towards elders meant not talking back to those in authority. The teacher telling the child to verbalize her reactions more readily conflicted with her cultural viewpoint (Clauss-Ehlers & Lopez Levi, 2002).

Although most people think about verbal communication as what defines language, nonverbal communication also plays a key role in classroom communication (Gollnick & Chinn, 2002). Like verbal communication, nonverbal language reflects the cultural context of the speaker. Some cultures rely more upon the context in which the communication takes place. Context-dependent communication goes beyond the spoken word in an attempt to understand the nature of what is being said. The context-dependent communicator incorporates contextual factors in interpretations such as the emotion and physical movement associated with the message.

The all too common question "How are you?" provides an excellent example of context-dependent vs. verbal-dependent interpretation of language. "How are you?" is a question Americans frequently ask one another in every day life. The expectation is that the individual being asked the question will simply say "Fine" regardless of his or her mood. The response is acknowledged and the two parties move on.

The unexpected response is the individual who replies: "I don't feel great today, things aren't going well. I'd like to talk to you about it." Hence, the typical "How are you?" exchange is verbally-dependent because no matter how the respondent says "Fine" (i.e., even if said with a depressed tone), the initiator of the conversation takes the "Fine" reply at face value and continues about his or her business.

Nonverbal communication challenges educators to be context-dependent in their interpretation of the language systems that operate in the classroom. Physical proximity and facial expression are two such examples. Cultural groups differ in the amount of physical proximity that is deemed acceptable. For Latino communities it is common to greet one another with a kiss on the cheek or an embrace. In many European cultures it is customary to greet someone by placing a kiss on each cheek.

White Americans leave an average distance of twenty-one inches between themselves and others. Cultural groups such as Latin Americans, Arabs, and Southern Europeans, however, may experience this as being too distant (Gollnick & Chinn, 2002). It is important to explore these cultural differences with students. Students accustomed to greater proximity may find it difficult to engage in classroom discussions where peers are physically distant.

Facial expressions are another type of context-dependent communication. In mainstream American society, eye contact is associated with assertiveness, listening, and being responsive. Many U.S. teachers expect their students to look at them when they are speaking. Some cultural groups, however, view direct eye contact as a sign of disrespect. Instead, the child is to show respect by looking down at the floor or away from the teacher. To do otherwise is considered an inappropriate challenge. The risk for the student is that the teacher misinterprets the indirect eye contact as disrespectful and inattentive.

It is important to mention within-group differences when nonverbal communication is discussed. There is no cookbook approach for understanding cultural nuances associated with nonverbal communication. Not everyone from one group communicates nonverbally in a particular way. Your task is to understand both the individual and cultural differences associated with a student's nonverbal communication.

Working with English Language Learners in the Classroom

As many as 10,000 known languages exist throughout the world (Crystal, 1997). Language differences include dialect, accent, and language microcultures. Sign language, for instance, is a linguistic microculture that involves a "system of vocal sounds and/or nonverbal systems by which group members communicate with one another" (Gollnick & Chinn, 2002, p. 247). American Sign Language (ASL) is considered a legitimate language with its own grammatical structure, syntax, and vocabulary (Gollnick & Chinn, 2002). While a focus on diverse language microcultures is beyond the scope of this chapter, you are encouraged to seek out additional information about these important language systems. The remainder of Chapter 6 will focus on English Language Learners (ELL).

As a contemporary educator, you will have a student in your class whose first language is not English. State-reported data indicate that 5,112,081 ELL students were enrolled in grades pre-K through 12 in public schools during the 2003-2004 academic year. This number represents almost 10.3% of total school enrollment in U.S. public schools. These statistics show a significant increase from earlier years. In 1993-1994, ELL enrollment was 3,552,497 (Office of English Language Acquisition, Language Enhancement, & Academic Achievement for Limited Proficient Students; National Clearinghouse for English Language Acquisition & Language Instruction for Educational Programs, n.d.).

Despite the increase in ELL students, there is ongoing controversy about bilingual education. In 1985, Secretary of Education William Bennett claimed bilingual education programs did not work. He argued that bilingual education put too much emphasis on the student's language of origin that interfered with teaching English (Bennett, 1985). While many of his proposed bilingual education changes were not implemented, the Title VII reauthorization of 1988 had clear implications for the state of bilingual education. Specifically, Title VII stated that federal initiatives could direct up to 25% of funds to English-only programs for students with limited English proficiency (Escamilla, 1989).

What is commonly known as the English Only movement refers to people who want to make English the official language of the United States (Escamilla, 1989). Support for the English Only movement is reflected in initiatives such as California Proposition 227 that passed in 1998. Proposition 227 says bilingual education does not work and puts an end to it in California. The policy requires that ELL students participate in sheltered English immersion programs for one year with instruction given in English. Students are transferred to mainstream English classes upon completion of their year (Unz & Tuchman, 1998). Those who oppose Proposition 227 say it lacks empirical support and does not work. Opponents agree it is important to learn English but advocate for bilingual education programs that incorporate both the language of origin and English.

The term bilingual education itself is often misunderstood. Bilingual education refers to using two languages for instructional purposes. The goal of bilingual education is not necessarily to teach a second language like English. Rather, the objective is to help children learn in their language of origin and *reinforce* that learning through the use of a second language like English (Gollnick & Chinn, 2002).

Gollnick and Chinn (2002) discuss two current approaches to bilingual education: the transitional approach and the maintenance approach. The transitional approach is an assimilationist approach. This approach says that bilingual education should help students shift from the language used at home to the predominant language used in the society. The goal of this approach is for students to become fully fluent in the new language. Maintaining the language of origin is not a priority.

The maintenance approach says that students should learn the new language but also maintain their language of origin. Students become bilingual and bicultural and neither language takes priority. Many bilingual educators prefer the maintenance approach. Most programs are transitional, however, due to the cost of maintenance programs and the lack of bilingual personnel.

Bilingual education is often confused with English as a Second Language (ESL) programs. ESL programs use English only in both teaching and instruction. The goal of ESL programs is for people to become fluent in English as quickly as possible.

Bilingual education is an excellent way to achieve cognitive development for bilingual students. It provides an equal educational opportunity, a transition for bilingual students, promotes bicultural efficacy, promotes intercultural relations, and offers educational reform (Clauss, 1998; Gollnick & Chinn, 2002). ELL students learn English content well when educational services meet their cultural and linguistic needs, instruction is provided in the language of origin as a foundation for instruction in English, and teachers spend adequate time on course material (Thomas & Collier, 1997).

Classroom Strategies

In *Working with English language learners: Strategies for elementary and middle school teachers*, Zehler (1994) presents five excellent instructional elements that facilitate learning among ELL students. These are presented below.

The classroom should be predictable and accepting of all students says that ELL students should be treated fairly and as individuals (Zehler, 1994). Acceptance means that you understand the student's individual and cultural diversity. Not all students from a particular culture will experience that culture in the same way.

Activities should be structured, predictable, and reflect the teacher's expectations of his or her students. Making classroom life predictable includes helping students understand what is expected of them (Zehler, 1994; See *Diversity Training Activity 6.1*).

Instructional activities should maximize opportunities for language use. Language expression is critical for learning among both native-English speakers and ELL students. Verbal abilities such as talking through ideas, raising questions, and being critical in arguments all develop higher order thinking. Maximizing opportunities for language usage means that you pose questions that extend and create new knowledge. Part of this process is to allow for ongoing dialogue in the classroom. One strategy is to organize cooperative learning groups where students communicate with one another to accomplish specific goals (Zehler, 1994).

Verbal and written activities also help students develop their English capability. As opportunities for language usage are provided, it is important to remember that correcting errors is not the focus. This is not to say that errors are never to be corrected, but that you are sensitive to the fact that ongoing corrections are intrusive. Modeling language usage and providing written responses is more sensitive than constantly correcting your students (Zehler, 1994).

Instructional tasks should involve students as active participants. A discovery process occurs when students are active classroom participants. Active students develop their own questions, hypotheses, and work in teams to come up with findings. These activities help ELL students build their knowledge of specific content areas and feel confident about moving from one language to the next.

Cooperative learning is another strategy that is sensitive to ELL students. In cooperative learning students learn from one another through tasks that they complete in small or large groups. Cooperative learning decreases the pressure of being singled out for class participation because the entire group contributes (See *Diversity Training Activity 6.1*). Cooperative learning exposes students to the range of English proficiency among their classmates and results in peer modeling and mentorship.

Instructional interactions should provide support for student understanding. Just as students need to be responsible for their learning, teachers need to meet that ownership with support and empathy. It is recommended that you adapt your use of the English language to the students' level of proficiency. Strategies include speaking at a slower pace, providing clear explanations of language usage, avoiding the use of jargon, and breaking down complex sentences into simpler structures (Zehler, 1994).

Using the language of origin also provides support. If you speak the same language as your students, you can use your linguistic ability to help explain course material. Use of nonlinguistic material is another way to promote understanding. Materials like graphics or outlines can help highlight a concept or idea.

Instructional content should utilize student diversity. The cultural backgrounds of ELL students add to the life of the classroom. Both ELL students and English speakers can share cultural experiences and traditions. For this process to work, diversity initiatives must be integrated throughout the curriculum rather than "assigned" to special designated days. These efforts will help students recognize that they are valued and taken seriously. It will let them engage in course content that reflects their life experience.

DIVERSITY TRAINING ACTIVITY 6.1

STUDENT SCENARIO:
SPECIAL EDUCATION OR LANGUAGE TRANSITION

RATIONALE

Some educators lack the skill and knowledge needed to accurately assess the educational needs of ELL students. As a result, ELL students risk being inappropriately placed in special education classes. The following *Diversity Training Activity* deals with the question of appropriate placement. The goal of this experience is to heighten your awareness of the potential pitfalls associated with the issue of placement for ELL students.

STEPS TO IMPLEMENTATION

1. Your instructor will divide the class into small groups of 5 to 6 students each.
2. Read and review the scenario presented below:

Anthony is a 6-year-old boy who has started first grade. He recently immigrated to the U.S. with his family, making the journey from Ecuador just 18 months earlier. Anthony's parents value education and enrolled him in a day care center at age 5. The day care provided informal educational experiences, interaction with children from ages 1 to 5, and good supervision. Both Spanish and English were spoken at the day care center. Spanish is the dominant language spoken in Anthony's home.

Anthony's enrollment in the first grade at his neighborhood public school is the first time he has been in a formal educational environment. Anthony finds the setting quite different from day care. Assignments are highly structured and all class content is conducted in English. At times the English language seems to be spoken so quickly that Anthony has difficulty following coursework. Frequently he turns to his friend who is fluent in Spanish and English and asks her to translate what the teacher has said into Spanish.

Anthony is also expected to be an active class participant. Students are rewarded for raising their hands, giving responses, and even disagreeing with one another. This approach causes great anxiety for Anthony. He is a shy child and fears that students will make fun of his limited English if he participates. Anthony tries to manage his concerns by being as quiet in class as he possibly can. Other than the conversations and translations from his fully bilingual neighbor, Anthony tries to be invisible, hoping the teacher will forget about him.

Anthony's grades begin to drop over the next several months. He has difficulty with spelling and math simply because he cannot understand the directions that are written in English. Parents are supposed to help their children with "family homework" every night but Anthony's parents cannot read English. Interestingly, when Anthony is asked to spell a word or complete an assignment in Spanish, he does quite well—he never makes a spelling mistake and completes math assignments to their fullest.

Anthony's teacher feels the first grade class is not appropriate for him at this time. She believes that Anthony's low verbal ability, reticent involvement, and lack of participation suggest he has some type of learning disability. The teacher has spoken to the school principal and Anthony's parents and recommended a special education placement. Anthony's parents are scared and upset. They feel their son is quite capable and simply undergoing the cultural change of adjusting to a new language, new country, and new educational environment.

3. Talk about your reaction to the above scenario in your small group.
4. Answer the discussion points below with the entire class.

DISCUSSION POINTS

You are the school principal presented with this scenario. Consider the following questions as you grapple with how to respond to Anthony's situation:

1. What will you say to Anthony's parents? His teacher?
2. Should Anthony stay in the first grade or be transferred to a special education classroom?
3. What resources and assessment measures will help you make your decision?
4. What do you think the school's position should be in this situation?

DIVERSITY TRAINING ACTIVITY 6.2
YOUR APPROACH TO BILINGUAL EDUCATION

RATIONALE

The purpose of *Diversity Training Activity 6.2* is to have you think about the type of bilingual education you feel is most helpful for future ELL students. Current controversy has made bilingual education a national debate. This *Diversity Training Activity* is designed to help you analyze and verbalize your perspective about this critical contemporary issue.

STEPS TO IMPLEMENTATION

1. *Diversity Training Activity 6.2* can be conducted in small groups or with your entire class.
2. Consider the questions below as you critically analyze your perspective on bilingual education.

DISCUSSION POINTS

1. What approach best ensures that ELL students learn course content: the transitional approach, the maintenance approach, immersion in an ESL program, or participation in an English-only classroom?
2. What influences your perspective?
3. What are the advantages and disadvantages associated with your view?
4. What strategies will make you an effective teacher when working with ELL students?

NOTEBOOK SECTION FOR CHAPTER 6
LANGUAGE IN THE CLASSROOM

I. CONCEPTS/THEORIES

II. CLASSROOM OBJECTIVES

_____

_____

_____

_____

_____

_____

_____

_____

_____

_____

_____

_____

_____

_____

_____

_____

_____

_____

_____

_____

_____

_____

_____

_____

_____

_____

_____

_____

_____

III. BEST PRACTICES (HOW TO IMPLEMENT THOSE OBJECTIVES IN THE CLASSROOM)

_____

_____

_____

_____

_____

_____

_____

_____

_____

_____

_____

_____

_____

_____

_____

_____

_____

_____

_____

_____

_____

_____

_____

_____

_____

_____

WEB RESOURCES

- The University of Southern California Center for Multilingual Multicultural Research has a Website that presents a list of useful links and resources for teachers. Some of the links include the BUENO Center for Multicultural Education, a Bilingual Families Web page, and ESL/Bilingual Lesson Plans and Resources. A section of the Website also provides a listing of full text articles and resources. The title of each full text article is provided along with a document summary. The link for this Website is:
  http://www-bcf.usc.edu/~cmmr/BEResources.html
- Paso Partners has a Website that features an instructional program that integrates mathematics, science, and language arts for English/Spanish bilingual primary-grade children. The site provides resources for elementary school teachers that include a curriculum plan, instructional strategies, and assessment procedures. Lesson units are provided for K-3rd grades on a variety of different topics. Each unit includes English and Spanish versions of the topic. Topics for kindergarteners, for instance, include Five Senses (Los Cinco Sentidos), Spiders (Arañas), and Dinosaurs (Los Dinosaurios). Those for third graders include Matter (La Materia), Sound (El Sonido), and Simple Machines (Las Máquinas Sencillas). Each topic has a lesson overview, teacher background information, lesson focus, an objective grid, and the actual lessons. The link for this site is:
  http://www.sedl.org/scimath/pasopartners/welcome.html

REFERENCES

Bennett, W. (1985). *Address to the Association for a Better New York.* Washington, DC: United States Department of Education.

Clauss, C.S. (1998). Language: The unspoken variable in psychotherapy practice. *Journal of Psychotherapy, 35*(2), 188-196.

Clauss-Ehlers, C.S., & Lopez Levi, L. (2002). Working to promote resilience with Latino youth in schools: Perspectives from the U.S. and Mexico. *International Journal of Mental Health Promotion, 4*(4), 14-20.

Crystal, D. (1997). *The Cambridge encyclopedia of language* (2nd ed.). Cambridge, UK: Cambridge University Press.

Dana, R.H. (1996). Culturally competent assessment practice in the United States. *Journal of Personality Assessment, 66*(3), 472-487.

Escamilla, K. (1989). *A brief history of bilingual education in Spanish.* Charleston, WV: ERIC Clearinghouse on Rural Education and Small Schools. (ERIC Document Identifier No. ED308055). Retrieved May 10, 2005, from http://www.ericdigests.org/pre-9211/brief.htm

Gollnick, D.M., & Chinn, P.C. (2002). *Multicultural education in a pluralistic society* (6th ed.). Upper Saddle River, NJ: Merrill Prentice Hall.

Javier, R.A. (1995). Vicissitudes of autobiographical memories in a bilingual analysis. *Psychoanalytic Psychology, 12*(3), 429-438.

Office of English Language Acquisition, Language Enhancement, & Academic Achievement for Limited Proficient Students; National Clearinghouse for English Language Acquisition & Language Instruction for Educational Programs (n.d.). *AskNCELA No. 1*. Retrieved May 10, 2005, from http://www.ncela.gwu.edu/expert/faq/011eps.htm

Thomas, W., & Collier, V. (1997). *School effectiveness for language minority students.* Fairfax, VA: George Mason University.

Unz, R.K., & Tuchman, G.M. (1998). *Initiative statute: English language education for children in public schools.* Palo Alto, CA: Author.

Zehler, A. (1994). Working with English language learners: Strategies for elementary and middle school teachers. NCBE Program Information Guide Series, 19. Retrieved November 13, 2001 from http://www.ncbe.gwu.edu/ncbepubs/pigs/pig19.htm

Chapter 7

Working with Diverse Families: Parental Partnership in Education

The role of parental partnership in student academic success is receiving increasing attention in the literature (Cotton & Wikelund, 1989). Research highlights the fact that learning extends beyond the classroom and includes home and community environments. Identifying how you define family is a good first step towards working with parents. Complete *Diversity Training Activity 7.1* to begin this process. This activity will help you recognize the different definitions people have for the term "family." Family is defined here as "those persons who are biologically and/or psychologically related whom historical, emotional, or economic bonds connect and who perceive themselves as a part of a household" (Gladding, 2002, p.6).

It is also important to understand cultural aspects of family systems such as marriage forms, kinship relations, marital residential choice, family authority, and family values (Tseng & Hsu, 1979). Some cultures make no distinction between blood or biological relatives and non-family members. In the Latino culture, for instance, the *madrina* and *padrino* (i.e., godmother and godfather) are considered part of the family even when there is no biological tie. This differs from traditional Chinese family systems that make a strong distinction between maternal and paternal sides of the family.

The Importance of Parental Outreach

A common question about the topic of parental partnership is: "Why reach out to parents and families when the child is the educator's primary responsibility?" (Note that parent as it is used here also refers to caregiver and guardian). Developing an alliance with parents results in greater student learning. Research overwhelmingly shows that positive family involvement leads to higher grades, higher test scores, better attendance, more completed homework, a positive attitude, higher graduation rates, and being more likely to go to college (Henderson & Berla, 1994). Three factors over which parents have authority--student absenteeism, variety of reading materials in the home, and excessive television watching--account for 90% of the difference in the average state by state performance of 8th grade math test scores in 37 states and Washington, D.C. (Barton & Coley, 1992). These findings suggest that differences in achievement are largely due to home practices. The good news for the educator is that academic improvement can result from having parents make sure their children attend school regularly, encourage their children to read at home, and turn off the television (Barton & Coley, 1992).

Research also indicates that what the family does at home is more important to student success than family income or level of education (Walberg, 1984). Work with your families so they understand the extent to which home practices enhance academic success. The more you believe working with parents is important, the more your parents will recognize their contribution to their child's academic success.

Let families know that involvement in their child's education is a critical long-term investment. In 1996, the annual earnings of young adults between the ages of 25 to 34 who did not graduate from high school were 31% lower for males and 36% lower for females with a high school diploma (U.S. Department of Education, 1999). Males with a college education earned 54% more and females with a college education earned 88% more than peers with a high school diploma only (U.S. Department of Education, 1999).

The general public supports greater involvement in family learning. 40% of parents nationwide think they are not dedicating enough time to their child's education (Finney, 1993). Teachers say that strengthening parental involvement should be a top priority for public education (Louis Harris & Associates, 1993). Students also want more parent involvement. 72% of 10 to13-year-old-students want more time to talk with their parents about schoolwork. 48% of 14 to 17-year-olds want to spend more time with their parents in general (National Commission on Children, 1991). These findings defy the myth that adolescents shun parental involvement. Rather, they highlight the fact that youth want to feel their parents' presence as they transition through adolescence.

Barriers to Parental Partnership

If parental partnership is critical to student success, why isn't it happening more? Several barriers highlight the many struggles parents face (Ballen & Moles, 1994). Time is one issue that is particularly relevant for dual career families, single parent families, and parents with more than one job. Striking a balance between work and family life is especially challenging. 66% of employed parents with children under the age of 18 say they do not have enough time for their children (Families and Work Institute, 1994).

Uncertainty about how to promote academic success is another barrier. Many parents feel they don't know how to help their children learn (The National Commission on Children, 1991). Some parents had bad experiences with school themselves and feel suspicious and intimidated by the educational process. Others want more time to help their children with homework but need guidance from their child's teacher (Epstein, 1987). Teachers themselves want training about how to facilitate parent involvement.

Cultural barriers can interfere with the development of parental partnerships. Some immigrant families may not understand English and the school may offer limited translation services. Undocumented families may fear deportation if they develop a close relationship with the school and their status becomes known. Families may have different views on schools and their role. For instance, some families may consider parental involvement to be disrespectful of the teacher's authority. It is important for schools to have policies on parental partnership and provide resources that encourage liaisons between parents and the school community.

Parental Partnership with Diverse Families

Cultural engagement is one way to work with diverse families (Tseng & Hsu, 1979). Cultural engagement says it is important to engage families in a way that reflects their cultural background (Tseng & Hsu, 1979). Questions to consider are how family members greet one another socially and culturally sanctioned ways that members communicate with one another. Critical to cultural engagement is the ability to develop rapport with families from their cultural frame of reference.

Gearing to the existing hierarchy is a second aspect of the Tseng and Hsu (1979) model. Your students may have different family structures than you do. Your job is to figure out hierarchical patterns of authority and work within their parameters. For instance, if the grandmother plays a key caregiver role in your student's life, it is important to invite her to parent-teacher conferences. This values the grandmother's role. Your student's academic success is supported since the grandmother is the one at home who helps your student with his homework.

Culturally appropriate communication is a third component of the Tseng and Hsu (1979) model. Culturally appropriate communication refers to communication patterns formed by cultural subsystems. Eye contact is one example of culturally-based nonverbal communication. In the Latino community, for instance, a woman who engages in extended direct eye contact with a man is thought to be flirting. A female teacher may think direct eye contact with a Latino father shows that she is being responsive when in fact this behavior risks offending the family.

Culturally relevant exposure of private matters is another consideration (Tseng & Tsu, 1979). This issue concerns who should be in the room when difficult issues are presented. Sensitivity, respect, and familiarity with the family are needed to determine who should be present when a student's struggles are discussed.

The ability to clarify your approach, procedure, and goal makes families aware of your role and expectations (Tseng & Tsu, 1979). Families come to schools with different perspectives about what their involvement should be. For instance, some Latino immigrant families will shy away from meeting with teachers because they consider parental questioning a sign of disrespect. Staying away from school is done out of respect for the teacher's authority--the behavior does not reflect a lack of interest on behalf of the parents. Being clear means that your students' parents know the level of participation you expect from them. Give them permission to be involved. The following *Diversity Training Activities* aim to enhance your ability to develop school-family partnerships.

DIVERSITY TRAINING ACTIVITY 7.1
HOW DO YOU DEFINE FAMILY?

RATIONALE

It is critical for you to grasp the heterogeneity of family composition in your work with students. *Diversity Training Activity 7.1* encourages you to explore how you define family. Being aware of your own assumptions about the definition of family will help you acknowledge the different ways that others define their families.

STEPS TO IMPLEMENTATION

1. Take a moment and write down how you define family. Include who makes up the members of your family in your definition.
2. Your instructor will ask participants to volunteer their definition of family.
3. Your instructor will write definitions on the board.

DISCUSSION POINTS

As you review the definitions of family presented by your classmates, note how many different definitions of family emerged from this brief exercise. The questions below form the focus of your discussion:

1. What are the similarities and differences among the definitions of family presented in class?
2. What do these differences suggest about extending your understanding of the term "family"?
3. What implications do these differences have for you in your role as an educator?

DIVERSITY TRAINING ACTIVITY 7.2

A CASE EXAMPLE: SUDS TO SUCCESS

RATIONALE

The Suds to Success program is offered at the Lincoln School Annex in New Brunswick, New Jersey. The aim of this program is to increase parental involvement so that students will perform better academically. A local business donated a washer/dryer that parents can use free of charge. Parents do their laundry at the school. While clothes are in the wash, parents have time to meet with teachers, the principal, and school personnel to learn more about what is going on at school.

See http://www.njea.org/Issues/JuneSidebar.asp for more information about the Suds to Success program.

STEPS TO IMPLEMENTATION

1. Your instructor will divide the class into small groups of 5 to 6 students each.
2. Research the Suds to Success program in your small group.

DISCUSSION POINTS

The focus of your discussion is on innovative programs that promote parental partnership and academic success. Specific questions include:

1. What are your thoughts about the Suds to Success program?
2. In what ways does this program meet the promise of parental partnerships with schools?

3. What creative ideas can forge liaisons between schools and families?
4. How will you implement these initiatives in your school community?

DIVERSITY TRAINING ACTIVITY 7.3

SCHOOLS THAT PARTNER WITH FAMILIES

RATIONALE

Diversity Training Activity 7.3 is designed to help you explore current school-family partnership initiatives. You will conduct research on parental partnership practices at a nearby school. Investigating the real life experiences of school personnel engaged in these efforts gives you greater insight about best practices for parental partnership. The goal of *Diversity Training Activity 7.3* is to encourage you to think about how to involve families in education.

STEPS TO IMPLEMENTATION

1. Select the school where you will conduct your research.
2. Set up appointments with the principal, teachers, and other school personnel to talk about current efforts that involve families in the life of the school.
3. Schedule a second set of meetings to talk with parents about their involvement. You may visit a parent resource center, attend a seminar for parents, or interview parents about their experience.
4. Write a 4-page paper that presents what you learned.

DISCUSSION POINTS

Questions for discussion include:

1. How did the school you studied facilitate parental partnerships?
2. What themes emerged in the school's efforts to involve families?
3. Were you surprised at the level of parental partnership achieved at the school you studied? Why or why not?
4. How does what you observed influence your thoughts about working with families?

NOTEBOOK SECTION FOR CHAPTER 7

WORKING WITH DIVERSE FAMILIES:
PARENTAL PARTNERSHIP IN EDUCATION

I. CONCEPTS/THEORIES

_____

_____

_____

_____

_____

_____

_____

_____

_____

_____

_____

_____

_____

_____

_____

_____

_____

_____

_____

_____

_____

II. CLASSROOM OBJECTIVES

_____

_____

_____

_____

_____

_____

_____

_____

_____

_____

_____

_____

_____

_____

_____

_____

_____

_____

_____

_____

_____

_____

_____

_____

_____

III. BEST PRACTICES (HOW TO IMPLEMENT THOSE OBJECTIVES IN THE CLASSROOM)

_____

_____

_____

_____

_____

_____

_____

_____

_____

_____

_____

_____

_____

_____

_____

_____

_____

_____

_____

_____

_____

_____

_____

_____

_____

_____

_____

_____

_____

WEB RESOURCES

- The National Education Association (NEA) and the National Parent Teacher Association (PTA) have published four guides that focus on parental partnership for academic success. They are available online and include the following:
  - *Helping Your Student Get the Most Out of Homework*
  http://www.nea.org/parents/homework.html
  - *A Parent's Guide to Helping Your Child With Today's Math*
  http://www.nea.org/parents/math.html
  - *A Parent's Guide to Raising Scientifically Literate Children*
  http://www.nea.org/parents/science.html
  - *A Parent's Guide to Improving School Achievement*
  http://www.nea.org/parents/achieve.html
- The School Improvement Research Series has an article entitled *Parent Involvement in Education* (Cotton & Wikelund, 1989). The authors review the literature and explore the influence of parent involvement on student achievement, the most effective types of involvement, and working with parents from diverse communities. The link for this Web page is:
  http://www.nwrel.org/scpd/sirs/3/cu6.html

REFERENCES

Ballen, J., & Moles, O. (1994). *Strong families, strong schools: Building community partnerships for learning.* Washington, DC: National Family Initiative, U.S. Department of Education.

Barton, P.E., & Coley, R.J. (1992). *America's smallest school: The family.* Princeton, NJ: Educational Testing Service.

Cotton, K., & Wikelund, K. (1989). *Parent involvement in education.* NW Regional Educational Laboratory, School Improvement Research Series. Retrieved April 6, 2005, from http://www.nwrel.org/scpd/sirs/3/cu6.html

Epstein, J.L. (1987). What principals should know about parent involvement. *Principal,* January: 6-9.

Families and Work Institute. (1994). *Employers, families, and education: Facilitating family involvement in learning.* New York, NY: Author.

Finney, P. (1993). The PTA/Newsweek national education survey. *Newsweek.* May 17.

Gladding, S.T. (2002). *Family therapy: History, theory, and practice.* Upper Saddle River, NJ: Pearson Education, Inc.

Henderson, A. T., & Berla, N. (1994). *A new generation of evidence: The family is critical to student achievement.* St. Louis, MO: Danforth Foundation and Flint, MI: Mott (C.S.) Foundation.

Louis Harris, & Associates. (1993). *Metropolitan life survey of the American teacher 1993: Violence in American public schools.* New York, NY: Author.

National Commission on Children. (1991). *Speaking of kids: A national survey of children and parents.* Washington, DC: Author.

Tseng, W., & Hsu, J. (1979). Culture and psychotherapy. In A.J. Marsella, R.G. Tharp, & T, J. Ciborowski (Eds.), *Perspectives on cross-cultural psychology* (pp. 333-345). New York, NY: Academic Press.

U.S. Department of Education (1999). *Annual earnings of young adults, by educational attainment* (NCES Publication No. 1999-009). Washington, DC: Author.

Walberg, H. J. (1984). Improving the productivity of American schools. *Educational Leadership, 41*, 19-77.

Section 3

Dimensions of Difference: Gender

Chapter 8
Gender

Gender is a construct we use when we talk about whether someone is male or female. Banks and McGee Banks (2005) define gender as "a category consisting of behaviors that result from the social, cultural, and psychological factors associated with masculinity and femininity within a society. Appropriate male and female roles result from the socialization of the individual within a group" (p. 450). Gender has social significance as boys and girls take on roles based on societal perceptions of masculinity and femininity. Gender roles develop from the ways that males and females are socialized into their gender group.

Diversity Training Activity 8.1, Memories of Gender Difference, is designed to encourage reflection about how people are socialized into gender roles. Self-awareness about the gender role socialization process is a critical starting point for understanding how gender bias and inequity play out in the classroom. Take a moment and complete *Diversity Training Activity 8.1.*

Gender Identity

Gender role socialization directly relates to gender identity. Gender identity refers to "an identity assigned to a particular individual on the basis of culturally-specific behaviors, attitudes, and feelings expected of one sex or the other; these can be classified into masculine and/or feminine behavior-affective patterns" (University of Minnesota, n.d.). Traditional gender identification for boys, for instance, focuses on independence and achievement. In contrast, traditional gender identity for girls values nurturance and passivity.

Psychologists like Sandra Bem argue that individuals who combine both masculine and feminine characteristics in their gender identities cope better than those with exclusively male or female gender identities. Bem (1974, 1995) says that individuals can internalize masculine and feminine characteristics. She uses the term androgynous to describe a gender identification that incorporates both masculine and feminine traits.

Bem (1974) developed a scale to explore whether someone has a predominantly male, female, or androgynous gender identification. In her *Bem Sex-Role Inventory* ([BSRI]; Bem, 1974) subjects respond to a sixty-item instrument. Items include twenty personality traits that reflect masculine attributes, twenty personality traits that reflect feminine attributes, and twenty personality traits that reflect androgynous attributes. Participants respond to items on a 7-point scale in which 7=*Always or Almost Always True* and 1=*Never or Almost Never True*. The Bem scale has been used in studies that explore how gender identity relates to concepts like resilience and self-efficacy (Bem 1974; Cook, 1985; Clauss-Ehlers, Yang, & Chen, 2005).

Gender Bias in Education

The terms mentioned above set the backdrop for discussion about gender bias in education. Gender bias refers to gaps in educational resources, attainment, performance, and access that are determined by gender. Gender bias is the focus of Chapter 8 as it is not always included in discussions about educational equity. A content analysis of journal articles on educational reform, for instance, found that only 1% of publications discussed gender bias (Sadker, Sadker, & Steindam, 1989). Research also shows that teachers receive less than two hours of training on the topic (American Institutes for Research, 1998). The indicators of gender bias discussed below are ability in math, science, and reading, SAT scores, self-esteem, and gender differences in classroom interaction (Basile, 1995).

Ability in math, science, and reading. Much of the gender bias literature focuses on math proficiency. Gender bias in science is the next area that is most researched followed by reading (Basile, 1995). While girls and boys start kindergarten from the same academic vantage point, by grade twelve girls lag behind boys in math and science (Entwisle, Alexander, & Olson, 1994). Boys take more advanced mathematics courses, are more likely to take all three core science courses (i.e., biology, chemistry, and physics), and receive higher scores on the National Assessment of Education Progress (NAEP) test of subject knowledge (American Institutes for Research, 1998). NAEP scores show that boys score highest in math, science, history, and geography while girls score highest in reading and writing (American Institutes for Research, 1998). While there is an increase in enrollment for girls in math and science, they still lag behind boys when it comes to taking advanced science and computer science classes (American Institutes for Research, 1998).

SAT scores. The SAT is a standardized test used for entrance to college. The SAT is a timed test with critical reading (formerly known as the verbal section), mathematics, and writing sections. Scholarships are often tied to scores on the SAT and the Preliminary Assessment Test (PSAT) that is taken during the junior year of high school. Research indicates that boys score higher than girls on math and verbal tests (American Institutes for

Research, 1998). PSAT scores for girls increased when the writing section was introduced in 1997.

Self-esteem. Educational achievement is also influenced by differences in self-esteem. Substantial research examines decreases in self-esteem among girls as they become adolescents. A central theme to this work is that some girls adopt traditional gender identities that value passivity and non-assertiveness during this transition (Rogers & Gilligan, 1988). Thus, at the very time that girls need to achieve to get into college, social pressures tell them they aren't valued for their accomplishments.

One study found that girls from diverse racial/ethnic backgrounds felt worse about themselves as they transitioned to high school (Wellesley College Center for Research on Women, 1992). 55% of White, 65% of African American, and 68% of Latina girls reported "being happy as I am" in elementary school. By the time they got to high school, these percentages had dropped to include only 22% of the White girls, 58% of African American girls, and 30% of Latinas.

Decreases in self-esteem coupled with increases in traditional gender-role identification relate to poor performance in math and science (Coley, 1989). These realities are further confounded by the fact that girls are at risk for a series of health and educational problems like depression, delinquency, substance abuse, and pregnancy (American Institutes for Research, 1998). 20% of girls report having been sexually or physically abused, 25% experience some symptoms of depression, and 25% do not receive necessary health care (American Institutes for Research, 1998).

Gender differences in classroom interaction is another indicator of gender bias (Basile, 1995). This refers to differential treatment based on gender. As early as kindergarten, boys learn to ask more questions in class than girls (Good, Slavings, Harel, & Emerson, 1987). Boys tend to be praised for their ability while girls are praised for polite behavior (Houston, 1985). Girls are called on less while boys are encouraged to be active class participants (Sadker & Sadker, 1994).

All of the above have implications for educational attainment and success. Unfair treatment puts girls at an academic disadvantage. They may get angry at being treated unfairly, become disengaged, or feel school work does not reflect their experience. The fact that girls are reinforced for not asking questions means they are not valued for being curious. Being rewarded for politeness sends the message that girls are valued for not causing problems rather than engaging in intellectual inquiry. This pattern of interaction sets girls up to focus on being "good girls" instead of being smart.

The Educator's Role

Your role as a multicultural educator is to be aware of how gender, gender identity, and gender bias play out in the classroom. The three *Diversity Training Activities* presented below are geared to foster a timely, equitable response to gender issues in class. *Diversity Training Activity 8.1, Memories of Gender Difference,* challenges you to examine how you learned about gender roles, how that learning plays out in your life, and how your gender identity influences classroom dynamics.

Diversity Training Activity 8.2, Recommendations for an Education Free of Gender Bias, presents strategies for gender-fair learning from the literature. These strategies encompass larger policy issues as well as classroom interventions. On a policy level it is recommended that schools and school districts focus on increasing the number of girls who enroll in physics, biology, and chemistry (American Institutes for Research, 1998). One classroom level strategy is for teachers to receive feedback about who they call on (i.e., boys, girls, or both) during class discussions.

Your role as a multicultural educator is to be responsive to instances of gender bias that arise in your school. Equitable intervention requires knowledge and awareness about the occurrence of gender bias along with the confidence and skill to intervene appropriately. *Diversity Training Activity 8.3, Student Scenario: Handling Gender Bias in the Classroom,* is a role-play activity that lets you practice your response to gender-based inequities.

DIVERSITY TRAINING ACTIVITY 8.1
MEMORIES OF GENDER DIFFERENCE

RATIONALE

Diversity Training Activity 8.1 builds on *Diversity Training Activity 2.3* as it advances awareness of emotional aspects of difference that, in this case, pertain to gender. The purpose of this activity is to have you process how you were socialized to be a boy or a girl, how you felt about this socialization experience, and who contributed to it (i.e., school, parents, and peers). As you share your story and listen to that of others, document the relevant themes experienced by group members in terms of their gender role socialization.

STEPS TO IMPLEMENTATION

1. Your instructor will organize the class into small groups of 5 to 6 participants.
2. Each participant will discuss memories associated with gender role socialization. The discussion questions presented below will help your group engage in this dialogue.
3. As you talk about how you learned to act like a boy or a girl, be sure to explore the feelings that came up for you during this time. Identify the common themes associated with the gender role socialization process as you listen to group members.

DISCUSSION POINTS

The main focus of discussion for *Diversity Training Activity 8.1* is to further awareness about the gender role socialization process. As you grapple with identifying what that experience was like for you, consider the following questions:

1. What did you learn about being a boy or a girl as a young child?
2. What was the social significance of being a boy or a girl?
3. Were there particular activities, events, or experiences that you associated with being a boy or a girl at a young age?
4. Are there activities, events, or experiences that you associate with being a man or a woman at this point in your life?
5. How did other people contribute to your sense of gender role (i.e., parents, friends, neighbors, extended family)?
6. How did your school contribute to your sense of gender role (i.e., during preschool, elementary, middle, high school, and at college/university)?
7. Were there occasions when you wanted to engage in activities and behaviors that conflicted with your "prescribed" gender role? How did you deal with these situations?
8. How did others react when you engaged in behaviors that conflicted with gender role expectations?
9. What feelings did you have about your gender role then? What feelings do you have about your gender role now?
10. How do you view your role as an educator dealing with issues of gender in the classroom?

DIVERSITY TRAINING ACTIVITY 8.2
RECOMMENDATIONS FOR A GENDER BIAS
FREE EDUCATION

RATIONALE

Gender bias is an all too common problem in contemporary classrooms. Your job as a multicultural educator is to address the possibility of gender bias and provide alternative strategies that promote equitable education. This does not mean that you pay selective attention to issues of gender bias once a year. A comprehensive approach means you work with school, district, and classroom environments on a regular basis. Table 8.1 describes strategies that promote gender fair education. Each strategy is listed along with its scope of influence (i.e., school-wide, district-wide, or classroom) and rationale. The purpose of *Diversity Training Activity 8.2* is to design a class project that reflects the goals of a gender equitable school, district, or classroom intervention.

STEPS TO IMPLEMENTATION

1. Review Table 8.1 and write a three-page paper that presents a school-wide, district-wide, or classroom intervention strategy that responds to one of the four indicators of gender bias discussed in this chapter.
2. Your paper should present a strategic plan to address the indicator you selected. Your proposed plan can be implemented on a macro level (i.e., school-wide, district-wide) or on a more micro basis (i.e., classroom based).
3. Your instructor will collect your assignments for review. Discuss the questions in the Discussion Points section with your classmates to start a dialogue about gender bias.

Table 8.1 Recommendations for a Gender Bias Free Education

Educational Strategy & Citation	Strategy Level (i.e., School-Wide, District- Wide, or Classroom)	Strategy Rationale
Increase the number of girls enrolled in core science courses: chemistry, biology, and physics (American Institutes for Research, 1998).	School-Wide, District-Wide & Classroom	Have girls increase their participation in core science classes to help decrease gender gaps in the sciences.
Make algebra 1 and geometry mandatory classes for all students (American Institutes for Research, 1998).	School-Wide, District-Wide & Classroom	Algebra 1 and geometry are mandatory courses to study math, science, engineering, and computer science in college. Making them mandatory decreases the gender gap as it prepares both girls and boys.
Teachers should encourage girls to take more difficult math and science classes like those at the Advanced Placement level (American Institutes for Research, 1998).	School-Wide, District-Wide & Classroom	Being encouraged to enroll in Advanced Placement math and science courses decreases the gender gap and gives girls the opportunity to earn AP credit in these areas.
Math and science gaps should be reported as early as elementary school instead of in junior high school (Basile, 1995).	School-Wide & District-Wide	This strategy is preventive. Early intervention can decrease gaps in math and science that start early on. Early intervention will help girls receive the support they need before they reach junior high.
Gender equity should be a valued part of teacher education and a focus for pre-service teacher training (American Institutes for Research, 1998).	Classroom & School-Wide	Undergraduate and graduate programs that train teachers must spend more time on the influence of gender bias on educational outcomes for all students.
Standardized tests should include a writing section to build upon girls' strengths in this area (American Institutes for Research, 1998).	District-Wide	Standardized tests that include a writing section build upon the strengths that girls bring to the testing experience. The result of this addition will likely be a decrease in score differences between boys and girls. This strategy also promotes greater educational access as test performance is often linked to prestigious scholarships.

Table 8.1 (continued) Recommendations for a Gender Bias Free Education

Educational Strategy & Citation	Strategy Level (i.e., School-Wide, District- Wide, or Classroom)	Strategy Rationale
Teachers and schools must address what interferes with student participation (American Institutes for Research, 1998).	School-Wide, District-Wide & Classroom	Efforts to enhance student participation must consider self-esteem, parental partnerships in education, and perceptions about the value of school participation.
Schools must address risk factors like violence and teenage pregnancy by taking a strengths-based approach (American Institutes for Research, 1998).	School-Wide, District-Wide & Classroom	The strengths-based approach builds on the resources and assets students bring to situations. It takes a proactive stance rather than blaming the student.
Eliminate instructional materials that support traditional sex roles. Provide children with a variety of role models (McCormick, 1994).	Classroom	This approach helps students unlearn traditional gender role socialization. Diverse role models provide students with true-to-life examples of alternative behaviors and ways of being.
Plan for classroom activities that involve collaboration between boys and girls (McCormick, 1994).	Classroom	Collaborative groups that include boys and girls expose each gender to the other and promote gender-based learning.
Do not engage in sex-segregating policies (i.e., boys against the girls) (McCormick, 1994).	Classroom	This approach only furthers the divide between genders and can entrench gender roles that are already engrained.

DISCUSSION POINTS

1. Based on your own experience, how relevant is gender bias in today's schools?
2. Which, if any, of the four indicators of gender bias did you encounter in your educational experience?
3. What did you learn from writing your strategic plan?
4. How do you view your role as an educator who has to deal with gender issues in the classroom?
5. What strengths will help you manage gender bias?
6. What weaknesses will challenge your efforts?

DIVERSITY TRAINING ACTIVITY 8.3

STUDENT SCENARIO: HANDLING GENDER BIAS IN THE CLASSROOM

RATIONALE

In *Diversity Training Activity 8.3* you role-play how to deal with gender bias in the classroom. Both veteran teachers and recent graduates grapple with how to deal with gender bias associated with ability in math, science, and reading, SAT scores, self-esteem, and gender differences in classroom interaction. This *Diversity Training Activity* will help you become aware of gender bias and how to manage it in educational contexts.

STEPS TO IMPLEMENTATION

1. Read the scenario below:

    You are a teacher who has started to teach an 8^(th) grade class mid-year. The regular teacher is out on maternity leave and you will be with the class until the summer break. Over the course of your first week you notice differences in participation. The boys are more verbal and apt to ask questions while the girls appear less involved. You are uncertain about the cause of this behavior but know class participation is an integral part of testing new knowledge. Class participation is also part of the final grade so it is in each student's academic best interest to contribute to classroom discussion.

2. Your instructor will divide the class into small groups of 5 to 6 participants each.

DISCUSSION POINTS

1. How do you understand what is going on in the classroom?
2. What strategies can you use to address indicators of gender bias in this situation?
3. How do you explain the lack of intervention before you started to teach this class?
4. What challenges and barriers do you expect to face? How will you deal with them?

NOTEBOOK SECTION FOR CHAPTER 8

GENDER

I. CONCEPTS/THEORIES

_____

_____

_____

_____

_____

_____

_____

_____

_____

_____

_____

_____

_____

_____

_____

_____

_____

_____

_____

_____

_____

_____

_____

_____

II. CLASSROOM OBJECTIVES

III. BEST PRACTICES (HOW TO IMPLEMENT THOSE OBJECTIVES IN THE CLASSROOM)

WEB RESOURCES

* The American Association of University Women (AAUW) has a Web page focused on their Girls and Education Series. *Growing Smart: What's Working for Girls in Schools* (Hansen, Walker, & Flom, 1995) presents strategies to promote academic success among girls. *How Schools Shortchange Girls: The AAUW Report* examines how girls in grades K-12 get a poorer education than their male counterparts (Wellesley College Center for Research on Women, 1992). Information about how to order AAUW reports is also provided. The direct link to this Web page is:
  http://www.aauw.org/research/girls_education/index.cfm
* The U.S. Department of Education has a search engine that provides a listing of relevant resources by topic. When the term "gender" is searched, resources and programmatic information are provided in areas like women's educational equity and the promotion of gender equity in education. The direct link to results for a search by gender is: http://www.ed.gov/searchResults.jhtml?oq=gender+bias&odq=gender+bi as&qt=Gender&rq=0&st=0&

REFERENCES

American Institutes for Research (1998). *Gender gaps: Where our schools still fail our children*. Washington, DC: American Association of University Women Educational Foundation.

Banks, J.A., & McGee Banks, C.A. *Multicultural education: Issues and perspectives* (5th ed. update). New York, NY: John Wiley & Sons, Inc.

Basile, K.C. (1995). Gender differences in K-12 education: What indicators are important? Report prepared for the Georgia Council for School Performance. Retrieved June 6, 2005, from http://www.arc.gsu.edu/csp/DownLoad/gender.pdf

Bem, S.L. (1995). Dismantling gender polarization and compulsory heterosexuality: Should we turn the volume up or down? *Journal of Sex Research, 32*(4), 329-333.

Bem, S.L. (1974). The measurement of psychological androgyny. *Journal of Consulting and Clinical Psychology, 42*, 155-162.

Clauss-Ehlers, C.S., Yang, Y.T., & Chen, W. (2005.). Resilience from childhood stressors: The role of cultural resilience, ethnic identity, and gender identity. Manuscript under review.

Coley, R.J. (1989). The gender gap. *Educational Testing Service, 2*(1), 2-8.

Cook, E.P. (1985). *Psychological androgyny*. New York, NY: Pergamon Press.

Entwisle, D.R., Alexander, K.L., & Olson, L.S. (1994). The gender gap in math: Its possible origins in neighborhood effects. *American Sociological Review, 59*, 822-838.

Good, T.L., Slavings, R.L., Harel, K.H., & Emerson, H. (1987). Student passivity: A study of question asking in K-12 classrooms. *Sociology of Education, 60*, 181-189.

Hanson, S., Walker, J., & Flom, B. (1995). *Growing smart: What's working for girls in schools*. Washington, DC: American Association of University Women Educational Foundation.

Houston, B. (1985). Gender freedom and the subtleties of sexist education. *Educational Theory, 35*(4), 359-369.

McCormick, T.M. (1994). *Creating the nonsexist classroom.* New York, NY: Teachers College Press.

Rogers, A., & Gilligan, C. (1988). *Translating girls' voices: Two languages of development.* Harvard University Graduate School of Education, Harvard Project on the Psychology of Women and the Development of Girls.

Sadker, D., & Sadker, M. (1994). *Failing at fairness: How America's schools cheat girls.* New York, NY: Scribner's.

Sadker, D., Sadker, M., & Steindam, S. (1989). Gender equity and education reform. *Educational Leadership, 46*(6), 44-47.

University of Minnesota (n.d.). Biology dictionary: Women's studies 3202. Retrieved June 7, 2005, from http://womenstudy.cla.umn.edu/courses/3202/vocab.html

Wellesley College Center for Research on Women (1992). *The American Association of Women Report: How schools shortchange girls.* Washington, DC: American Association of University Women Educational Foundation.

Chapter 9
Sexual Orientation and Youth

Controversies about homosexuality abound in our schools. Educators not familiar with the issues faced by lesbian, gay, bisexual, and transgender (LGBT) youth may not know how to provide adequate support. It is hoped that Chapter 9 will enhance your understanding about diverse sexual orientations. You can begin this process by completing *Diversity Training Activity 9.1*, the *Homophobia and Heterosexism Quiz*. The quiz provides a starting point for understanding some of the myths, misconceptions, and misinformation that relate to LGBT youth. Continue to read the chapter after you complete *Diversity Training Activity 9.1*.

The American Psychological Association Public Interest (APA, n.d.) defines sexual orientation as "one component of a person's identity, which is made up of many other components, such as culture, ethnicity, gender, and personality traits. Sexual orientation is an enduring emotional, romantic, sexual, or affectional attraction that a person feels toward another person. Sexual orientation falls along a continuum. In other words, someone does not have to be exclusively homosexual or heterosexual, but can feel varying degrees of attraction for both genders. Sexual orientation develops across a person's lifetime—different people realize at different points in their lives that they are heterosexual, gay, lesbian, or bisexual." Sexual behavior does not necessarily relate to sexual orientation (APA, n.d.). Adolescents and adults can identify as being homosexual or bisexual without having had sexual experience. Adolescents who have had sexual experiences with people of the same gender may not identify themselves as lesbian, gay, bisexual, or transgender. These behaviors reflect the experimentation that is characteristic of the adolescent years (APA, n.d.).

A heterosexual person is "some one who is physically and emotionally attracted to people of opposing genders; also referred to as 'straight.' For example, women who like men and men who like women" (Lesbian Gay Bi Trans Youth Line, n.d.). Someone who is homosexual is "physically and emotionally attracted to people of the same gender. Because the term 'homosexual' has been (and is) used medically, psychologically, and historically in derogatory, marginalizing and hurtful ways, many people prefer to use the terms lesbian, gay and bisexual" (Lesbian Gay Bi Trans Youth Line, n.d.).

The term lesbian refers to a woman who is physically and emotionally attracted to other women. The term gay refers to someone who "forms physical and emotional relationships with persons of the same gender. Gay can be used to talk about both men and women or more generally the 'gay community,' but commonly refers to men" (Lesbian Gay Bi Trans Youth Line, n.d.). The term bisexual refers to someone who is "attracted physically and emotionally, to persons of the same and different genders. Bisexuals are not necessarily attracted equally to both men and women and not always attracted to both men and women at the same time" (Lesbian Gay Bi Trans Youth Line, n.d.). The term transgender is a "self-identifying term for someone whose gender identity or expression differs from traditional gender roles. Transgender is also a political umbrella term in English-speaking North America to refer to everyone who crosses gender roles in one way or another" (Lesbian Gay Bi Trans Youth Line, n.d.). The term questioning refers to people who are uncertain about their sexual orientation or sexual identity.

Homophobia and Social Isolation

It is important to note that risk factors for LGBT youth occur in a homophobic context. Homophobia refers to "an irrational fear or hatred of same-sex attractions expressed through prejudice, discrimination, harassment or acts of violence (known as 'bashing')" (Lesbian Gay Bi Trans Youth Line, n.d.). While LGBT adolescents experience many of the same developmental trajectories and challenges as their heterosexual peers (i.e., academic achievement, social skills, and professional choice), the existence of homophobia means they also face prejudice and discrimination that occurs at home, school, and in the community. One study found that lesbian, gay and bisexual students were more likely to miss school because they were afraid, had been threatened, or had their property damaged (Garofalo, Wolf, Kessel, Palfrey, & Du Rant, 1998). These results speak to the isolation, rejection by peers, violence, and verbal abuse that LGBT youth experience.

Lack of support for LGBT youth leads to greater emotional distress, risky sexual behavior, substance use and abuse, and greater attempted suicide in (Garofalo, et al., 1998; Resnick et al., 1997). One study found that gay and lesbian youth were two to three times more likely to attempt suicide than their heterosexual peers (Gibson, 1989). Another study found that 29% of 137 gay and bisexual males between the ages of 14 to 21 attempted suicide (Rernafedi, Farrow, & Deisher, 1991). Almost 33% of the youth in this sample first attempted suicide during the year that they identified as being homosexual or bisexual (Rernafedi et al., 1991).

School Interventions

Supportive interventions are needed to end homophobia in schools. *Diversity Training Activity 9.2, Action Points and Resources for People Working to End Homophobia in Schools,* presents strategies schools can use to create a safe environment for LGBT youth. You are encouraged to review these interventions and think about how to implement them as a future educator. Teachers, administrators, and school counselors must be able to provide "1) support and affirmation, 2) knowledge and accurate information, 3) role modeling, and 4) the ability to be counselor and consultant/advisor" to meet the needs of LGBT youth (Reynolds & Koski, 1994, p. 295). Competencies that effectively address the experience of LGBT youth include listening, empathy, problem solving, and the ability to manage conflict and ambiguity. Because these issues are controversial, educators and school counselors must be willing to deal with homophobia, take risks, and handle challenges (Reynolds & Koski, 1994).

Diversity Training Activity 9.3, Video Snapshot: It's Elementary: Talking About Gay Issues in School (Chasnoff & Cohen, 1996), presents a video that examines school efforts to address the needs of LGBT youth. Reynolds and Koski (1994) discuss how the normal developmental turbulence of adolescence is heightened for LGBT youth who are faced with "adopting a sexual identity that is often considered abnormal, immoral, and pathological" (p. 294). Because LGBT teens frequently have no one to talk to, including their families, they feel alone and isolated. Some adolescents will keep these feelings secret while others will come out and tell someone about their identity. It is hoped that youth who are coming out can do so "in a way that will allow them to feel comfortable with their sexuality" (Reynolds & Koski, 1994, p. 295).

DIVERSITY TRAINING ACTIVITY 9.1
HOMOPHOBIA AND HETEROSEXISM QUIZ

RATIONALE

The quiz in Table 9.1a highlights many of the myths tied to homosexuality.

STEPS TO IMPLEMENTATION

1. Take the quiz presented in Table 9.1a.

2. Review the answers to quiz items with the entire class (See Table 9.1b for quiz responses).

Table 9.1a Homophobia and Heterosexism Quiz

Question	Response
1. Homosexuality was listed as a disorder until 1973.	True False
2. Low self-esteem and self-deprecating beliefs do not relate to problem-solving abilities.	True False
3. Internalized homophobia can affect how people feel about their sexual orientation, but does not affect other aspects of their identity.	True False
4. Heterosexism can become especially difficult for those who become aware of their homosexuality during pre, early, or middle adolescence.	True False
5. Suicide is the leading cause of death among LGBT youth.	True False
6. The challenges faced by LGBT youth are the same as those faced by other youth.	True False
7. There are no particular school competencies that school counselors need when working with LGBT youth.	True False
8. Teachers who want to end homophobia in schools should not assume heterosexuality.	True False
9. Gay and lesbian youth are two to three times more likely to attempt suicide in comparison to their heterosexual peers.	True False
10. The lack of support for LGBT youth results in greater emotional distress, risky sexual behavior, substance use and abuse, and more attempted suicides in comparison to heterosexual teens.	True False

Table 9.1b Answers to Homophobia and Heterosexism Quiz

1. True. The American Psychiatric Association listed homosexuality as a mental disorder until 1973 when groups that included psychologists, medical doctors, and gay and lesbian activists convinced the American Psychiatric Association it was inappropriate to include homosexuality in its list of diseases.

2. False. Low self-esteem and self-deprecating beliefs can impair problem-solving abilities and lead to poor decision-making.

3. False. Internalized homophobia can lead to a hatred of one's sexual orientation as well as hatred of other aspects of one's identity.

4. True. Heterosexism can be especially difficult for those who become aware of their homosexuality during pre, early, or middle adolescence as they are forced to cope with stigma at a time when coping resources are developmentally limited.

5. True. Suicide is the primary cause of death among LGBT youth (Gibson, 1989).

6. False. Challenges faced by gay, lesbian, and bisexual youth are not the same as those faced by other youth given a climate of homophobia and negative reactions.

7. False. Counselor competencies that effectively address the experience of LGBT youth include listening, empathy, problem solving, and the ability to manage conflict and ambiguity (Reynolds & Koski, 1994).

8. True. It is important that teachers use inclusive language and not assume heterosexuality among those with whom they work.

9. True. Gay and lesbian youth are two to three times more likely to commit suicide in comparison to their heterosexual counterparts. They may consist of as much as 30% of all suicides that occur among youth each year (Gibson, 1989).

10. True. Lack of support for LGBT youth results in greater emotional distress, risky sexual behavior, substance use and abuse, and more attempted suicide in comparison to heterosexual teens (Garofalo, et al., 1998; Resnick et al., 1997).

DISCUSSION POINTS

As you review the different answers to the quiz, discuss the following with your class:

1. What was your reaction to quiz answers?
2. What do quiz answers suggest about the myths associated with homosexuality?
3. How do you view your role as an educator working with LGBT students?

DIVERSITY TRAINING ACTIVITY 9.2

ACTION POINTS AND RESOURCES FOR PEOPLE WORKING TO END HOMOPHOBIA IN SCHOOLS

RATIONALE

Multicultural educators work to provide a safe, healthy learning environment for all students. LGBT youth face many challenges as they confront environments that are homophobic. LGBT adolescents can experience isolation, violence, and be bullied. *Diversity Training Activity 9.2* presents ten action points and resources designed to create an inclusive school environment. While the following list is in no way exhaustive of all the possibilities for school intervention, it provides an initial foundation from which to base your efforts.

STEPS TO IMPLEMENTATION

1. Your instructor will divide the class into small groups of 5 to 6 students each.
2. Discuss the action points and resources mapped out in Table 9.2 in your small groups.

DISCUSSION POINTS

1. What did you learn about your own biases after reading the ten action points?
2. What feelings do you have about implementing these action points in a school setting?
3. How do you view your role as an educator working to end homophobia in schools?
4. What other resources can help end homophobia in schools?

Table 9.2 What You Can Do: Ten Action Points and Resources for People Working to End Homophobia in Schools

1. Do Not Assume Heterosexuality	The constant assumption of heterosexuality renders gay, lesbian, bisexual and transgender (LGBT) people invisible. Such invisibility is devastating to the individual's sense of self. Both the school as an institution and its professionals must be inclusive in their language and attitudes. By reminding themselves that LGBT people are found on every staff, in every classroom, and on every team, faculty can "unlearn" heterosexism.
2. Guarantee Equality	LGBT members of the school community need to know that their schools value equality and that they are protected against discrimination. Schools should add sexual orientation and gender identity to their non-discrimination and harassment policies. In addition, sexual orientation and gender identity/expression should be included in multicultural and diversity statements as a way to communicate a commitment to equal treatment for all.
3. Create a Safe Environment	It is the school's obligation to take proactive measures to ensure that all members of its community have a right to participate without fear of harassment. Schools must make it clear that neither physical violence nor harassing language like "faggot" and "dyke" will be tolerated. Creating a "Safe Zone" program—displaying posters, stickers, and other literature encouraging acceptance—is a great way to communicate that your school is a safe environment for all.
4. Diversify Library and Media Holdings	The library is frequently the first place to which students turn for accurate sexuality and gender information. Too often, few or no works on LGBT issues are found there. Librarians and media specialists need to be sure their holdings are up to date and reflect the diversity of our world. Materials that reflect LGBT themes and authors should be prominently displayed and easily accessible to students seeking them. The library and media center should reflect LGBT holidays and events in their programming, and should strive to make sure that individual classroom libraries are similarly inclusive. The GLSEN Bookstore is a great online "one-stop shopping" resource for LGBT materials.
5. Provide Training for Faculty and Staff	School staff need to be equipped to serve all the students with whom they work, including LGBT students and children from LGBT families. Understanding the needs of LGBT youth/families and developing the skills to meet those needs should be expected of all educators regardless of personal or religious beliefs.
6. Provide Appropriate Health Care and Education	While being LGBT is not only a "health issue," health education on sexuality and sexually transmitted diseases should sensitively address the issues of LGBT people. Counselors and health staff should be particularly careful to make their sensitivity to LGBT issues clear. By educating themselves about related support services and agencies, and making pamphlets and other literature available, health professionals can provide for the needs of the LGBT students and families with whom they work.

Table 9.2 (continued) What You Can Do: Ten Action Points and
Resources for People Working to End Homophobia in Schools

7. Be a Role Model	Actions speak louder than words. The most effective way to reduce anti-LGBT bias is to consistently behave in ways that appreciate all human beings and condemn discrimination of any kind. Though both straight and LGBT students will benefit from having openly LGBT educators, coaches and administrators, staff members need not be "out" or LGBT themselves in order to be good role models. By demonstrating respectful language, intervening during instances of anti-LGBT harassment, and bringing diverse images into the classroom in safe and affirming ways, all staff members can be model human beings for the students with whom they work.
8. Provide Support for Students	Peer support and acceptance is the key to any student's feeling of belonging in the school. "Gay-Straight Alliances" (GSAs) offer students this sense of belonging as well as the chance to effect positive change in their schools. GSAs welcome membership from any student interested in combating anti-LGBT bias and raising awareness of heterosexism and diverse gender/sexual identities. There are currently over 1200 GSAs registered with GLSEN and countless more across the nation. Consider being a GSA advisor and helping students in your community to form a club that provides support, understanding and an avenue for promoting equality and school change.
9. Reassess the Curriculum	Educators need to integrate LGBT issues throughout the curriculum—not just in classes such as health education, but in disciplines such as English, History, Art and Science. Pre-existing curricula should be broadened to include LGBT images where appropriate (such as in studies of the Holocaust and Civil Rights Movement). Current events, popular music and film, and other media that include LGBT people and issues should be regularly discussed in class. Classroom libraries, story times, and assigned reading should be thoughtfully structured to include the full range of human diversity. Finally, educators should take advantage of "teachable moments," treating questions, comments and instances of name-calling as opportunities to educate students about LGBT people and issues. Children spend the majority of their time in class. As long as LGBT issues are seen as "special" and outside the classroom, students will continue to see LGBT people as marginal.
10. Broaden Entertainment and Extracurricular Programs	Extracurricular activities often set the tone for the community. Programs such as assemblies, film nights, and school fairs should regularly include content that reflects the diversity of our world. Special LGBT events and holidays such as LGBT History Month (October) and Pride Month (June) should be incorporated into school wide celebrations. Guest speakers and lectures that can inform the school community about the unique needs and accomplishments of LGBT people should be a regular part of school programming.

The above information is published with permission of GLSEN, the Gay, Lesbian and Straight Education Network. Their Web site is www.glsen.org

DIVERSITY TRAINING ACTIVITY 9.3

VIDEO SNAPSHOT:
IT'S ELEMENTARY: TALKING ABOUT GAY ISSUES IN SCHOOL (CHASNOFF & COHEN, 1996)

RATIONALE

The video *It's Elementary: Talking About Gay Issues in School* (Chasnoff & Cohen, 1996) focuses on the importance of talking about gay issues in educational settings. Teachers and school administrators share how they discuss the subject in age appropriate ways. The video addresses the misinformation that children receive from the media and how this shapes their images of homosexuality. Examples illustrate how educational systems successfully respond to stressors faced by homosexual youth such as depression and suicide. Student/teacher dialogues are presented throughout the video. The underlying theme of these discussions is respect for all.

STEPS TO IMPLEMENTATION

1. Your instructor can order *It's Elementary* by contacting the Women's Educational Media Website at http://www.womedia.org/whatwedo.htm
2. A 37-minute educational version of the film and study guide are available.
3. After watching the video, discuss the questions below with the entire class.

DISCUSSION POINTS

1. How do you feel about discussing LGBT issues in the classroom?
2. What activities can help students gain greater awareness and understanding about LGBT issues?
3. How can your lesson plans encourage students to learn about sexual orientation?

NOTEBOOK SECTION FOR CHAPTER 9
SEXUAL ORIENTATION AND YOUTH

I. CONCEPTS/THEORIES

_____

_____

_____

_____

_____

_____

_____

_____

_____

_____

_____

_____

_____

_____

_____

_____

_____

_____

_____

_____

_____

_____

_____

II. CLASSROOM OBJECTIVES

III. BEST PRACTICES (HOW TO IMPLEMENT THOSE OBJECTIVES IN THE CLASSROOM)

WEB RESOURCES

- The Lesbian Gay Bi Trans Youth Line Website provides a comprehensive listing of definitions, an online forum, and community links. The site focuses on issues that youth face as they grapple with questions related to sexual orientation. The link is:
  http://www.youthline.ca/definitions/gender.html
- The APA Public Interest has a Web page devoted to youth and sexual orientation from a school perspective. The page is specifically geared towards principals, educators, and school personnel. It discusses sexual orientation development, legal principles, and provides a listing of resources that schools may use. The link for this Web page is:
  http://www.apa.org/pi/lgbc/publications/justthefacts.html

REFERENCES

American Psychological Association, Public Interest (n.d.). *Just the facts about sexual orientation and youth: A primer for principals, educators and school personnel.* Retrieved April 11, 2005, from http://www.apa.org/pi/lgbc/publications/justthefacts.html

Chasnoff, D. (Director & Co-Producer), & Cohen, H. (Co-Producer). (1996). *It's elementary: Talking about gay issues in school* [Film]. San Francisco, CA: Women's Educational Media.

Lesbian, gay, bi, trans, youth line (n.d.). *Definitions.* Retrieved April 11, 2005 from http://www.youthline.ca/definitions/sexuality.html

Garofalo, R., Wolf, R.C., Kessel, S., Palfrey, J., & Du Rant, R.H. (1998). The association between health risk behaviors and sexual orientation among a school-based sample of adolescents. *Pediatrics, 101*(5), 895-902.

Gay, Lesbian & Straight Education Network. (2002, January 1.). *10 things educators can do to ensure that their classrooms are safe for all students.* Retrieved on May 26, 2005, from http://www.glsen.org

Gibson, P. (1989). Gay male and lesbian youth suicide. *Report of the secretary's task force on youth suicide* (pp. 110-142). Washington, DC: United States Department of Health and Human Services.

Rernafedi, G., Farrow, J., & Deisher, R. (1991). Risk factors for attempted suicide in gay and bisexual youth. *Pediatrics, 87,* 869-875.

Resnick, M.D., Bearman, P.S., Blum, R.W., Baumnan, K.E., Harris, K.S., Jones, J., Tabor, J., Beuhring, T., Sieving, R.E., Shew, M., Ireland, M., Bearing, L.H., & Udry, J.R. (1997). Protecting adolescents from harm: Findings from the National Longitudinal Study on Adolescent Health. *Journal of the American Medical Association, 278* (10), 823-832.

Reynolds, A.L., & Koski, M.J. (1994). Lesbian, gay and bisexual teens and the school counselor: Building alliances. *The High School Journal, 77,* 88-94.

Section 4

Other Challenges to Diversity

Chapter 10
Bullying in Schools

Bullying was once considered a normal, inevitable part of growing up. Boys hitting each other on the playground were shrugged off with the thought that "Boys will be boys." Girls excluding one another were considered to be engaging in a rite of passage to womanhood. National incidents such as the shootings at Columbine High School in Littleton, Colorado, however, have cast new light on the age-old problem of bullying. The shooters at Columbine High School were bullied by their classmates and staged their attack as an act of revenge against them.

Bullying has a major impact on U.S. educational systems. Each day in the U.S., 160,000 children stay home from school because they fear being bullied (Vail, 1999). Every 7.5 minutes bullying behavior occurs on America's playgrounds (Mestel & Groves, 2001). 15% of students are bullied or initiate bullying behavior on a regular basis. 80 to 90% of adolescents are bullied at least once during their years at school (American Psychological Association, 1999; Banks, 1997).

Bullying at school means that learning occurs in a culture of fear and intimidation. School personnel who fail to intervene exacerbate bullying. It is important that you know how to deal with bullying whether you teach preschool, elementary, middle, or high school. Chapter 10 explains the concept of bullying: how it operates, the nature of its large-scale influence, and what you can do about it.

Defining bullying is a first step towards understanding it. Bullying occurs "when one or more persons repeatedly say or do hurtful things to another person who has problems defending himself or herself" (U.S. Department of Health and Human Services [USDHHS], 2003, p. 4). Direct attacks and indirect attacks are two types of bullying behavior (Banks, 1997). Direct attacks include behaviors directed at the victim. Teasing, taunting, hitting, stealing, and threatening are all examples of direct attacks. Indirect attacks are behaviors that socially isolate a student through purposeful exclusion. Gossip, rumors, and excluding a student from interaction with peers exemplify indirect attack behaviors.

Bullying involves a consistent physical or psychological intimidation that occurs over time and creates a pattern of harassment and abuse (Banks, 1997; USDHHS, 2003). Bullying is not a normal part of growing up. It is not an act of "boys being boys" or "girls being girls."

Characteristics of bullies and victims. A bully is someone who "repeatedly uses force, either physical or non-physical, to shame, humiliate and dominate a victim" (Twemlow & Sacco, 2002, p. 170). Students who bully have the desire to be in control (Banks, 1997). They assert themselves by force or use threats to get what they want. Bullies can demonstrate aggression towards teachers and parents. They can be impulsive, hot tempered, and unable to tolerate frustration (USDHHS, 2003). Bullies can appear tough and show little sympathy towards their victims (USDHHS, 2003). Some studies indicate that parents, teachers, and caregivers may support bullying behavior by rewarding aggression and using inconsistent, severe force as a way to discipline (Banks, 1997). This type of modeling teaches the child to react to situations with aggression and antagonism.

Victims are "the target for the bully's force ...[who] can become depressed, hopeless, and enraged at the mockery" (Twemlow & Sacco, 2002, p. 170). Victims of bullying can become aggressive or suicidal. Victims often don't report being bullied because they fear the bully will retaliate. As a result, they live with the bullying in silence and get little support.

Long-term effects of being bullied include low self-esteem, poor academic performance, school drop out, and depression (Banks, 1997). A child who is bullied may believe she deserved it and blame herself for being a victim. These beliefs have a profound effect on self-concept that can last throughout the victim's life.

Bystanders and perceptions of bullying. Bystanders are "the audience for the bully-victim drama" (Twemlow & Sacco, 2002, p. 170). Bullies feel more powerful when a bystander is present to witness their actions. The bystander audience heightens the bully's sense of power and control. Some bystanders get a vicarious thrill from watching bullying behavior. A smaller percentage of bystanders have been abused themselves and are too frightened to get involved (Twemlow & Sacco, 2002).

Bystanders play a potentially powerful role in the bully/victim drama. Their actions can influence the outcome of bullying behavior. They can intervene to stop the bullying behavior, for instance, or walk away, leaving the bully without an audience.

Perceptions of bullying are more complex than expected. Students often think that victims of bullying are responsible for being bullied (Oliver, Hoover, & Hazler, 1994). Some even believe that being bullied will "toughen up" victims and teach them how to defend themselves.

Parents and teachers also play a role in the way that bullying is perceived and managed. Parents may be unaware of the extent of the problem and not discuss bullying with their children (Banks, 1997). Some students feel that getting adults involved is akin to tattle tailing and will only elicit more mistreatment from the bully.

Students share that teachers seldom or never talk to their classes about bullying (Banks, 1997). They attribute the lack of discussion to the perception among teachers that bullying is a harmless rite of passage. Some teachers even bully their students. One news article, for instance, talked about teachers who taunted the gay students in their class (The British Broadcasting Corporation [BBC] News, 1998).

The *Diversity Training Activities* below are designed to help you develop the skills needed to stop bullying rather than collude with it.

DIVERSITY TRAINING ACTIVITY 10.1
BULLYING OBSERVATION

RATIONALE

You may not have witnessed or experienced bullying behavior for some time. Perhaps you never were bullied or didn't see this behavior going on at your school. *Diversity Training Activity 10.1* is designed to make you more aware of bullying behavior by observing activities at a nearby school.

STEPS TO IMPLEMENTATION

1. Your task is to visit a school for a day. The developmental age of the school can range from preschool to high school. You are to spend the day with the same class and accompany students to all events that make up their daily activities. If the class goes to the playground or cafeteria, for instance, you will also go to these areas. This type of shadowing will help you recognize bullying as a school-wide problem that occurs in multiple settings.
2. Take notes that describe your observations of the bullying behavior, the response of victims, and the response of those who witness the aggression. Be thoughtful about the role of the school in anti-bullying efforts. How do teachers and school personnel respond when bullying occurs?

3. Upon your return, your instructor will divide the class into small discussion groups. Talk with your group about what you saw and how people responded to bullying behaviors. Come up with potential solutions about how schools can address bullying. Table 10.1 presents several strategies for dealing with bullies and victims.
4. After your small group meetings, share your responses with the entire class.

DISCUSSION POINTS

Consider the questions below in your small groups and when you talk with the entire class:

1. How prevalent was bullying in the school that you observed?
2. What did you notice about the victim's experience of being bullied?
3. What was the bystander's role?
4. Did teachers and school personnel intervene to stop the bullying?
5. If so, what did they do? If not, what were the outcomes of the bullying behavior? What would you have done?

Table 10.1 Teacher Strategies, Interventions, and School-Wide Approaches to Deal with Bullies and Victims

Teacher Strategies to Deal with Bullies & Victims	Interventions for Bullies & Victims	School-Wide Approaches
Incorporate the theme of bullying in your lesson plan.	Understand that there is a reason for the bully's behavior.	Take a school-wide zero tolerance approach to bullying.
Do not ignore the bullying behavior.	Counseling can help bullies understand the need to bully. Counseling can help victims deal with the aftermath of having been bullied.	Have a school-wide policy that spells out how school personnel will manage and investigate bullying reports.
Let both bully and victim know that you are taking action against the bullying behavior.	Monitor the bully's behavior. Check in with the victim to see how he or she is doing.	Have a clear school-wide policy that articulates how bullying situations will be resolved. Be sure that all school personnel and students are aware of what to expect from this policy.
Explore available resources for both bullies and victims.	Provide resources to the bully, the victim, and their parents.	Have a school-wide policy that advocates for school-family liaisons.

DIVERSITY TRAINING ACTIVITY 10.2
LEARNING TO INTERVENE WHEN
BULLYING OCCURS

RATIONALE

Teachers and school personnel may fail to intervene when bullying occurs because they do not know how to respond. You may have observed a lack of intervention in the schools that you visited. Not intervening makes the teacher a bystander instead of someone who promotes a safe school environment. *Diversity Training Activity 10.2* is a skill-building activity that addresses how to effectively intervene when bullying occurs. This activity will help you think through the position you will take when bullying occurs on your watch.

STEPS TO IMPLEMENTATION

1. Your instructor will organize the class into small groups of 5 to 6 students. Read the following scenario in your groups:

   Ann is 12-years-old and the leader of her school clique. The girls in Ann's group flock to her because she is both popular and feared. Ann teases and ostracizes any girl she dislikes. She even has a Website with nasty comments written about her classmates Nancy and Karen. Ann's name is not officially mentioned on the Website but everyone knows she created it.

   While supervising study hall, the teacher sees Ann and her friends Maria and Alicia approach the table where Nancy and Karen are seated. Ann starts to say mean comments to Nancy and Karen as her two friends look on and smile. Then Ann pushes Karen off the desk chair. Karen knocks her jaw on top of the desk as she falls to the floor. The impact of the fall dislodges part of her braces. Ann laughs loudly and kicks Karen's braces across the room.

2. Having read the scenario, engage in a role-play that acts out the discussion that follows among the teacher, Ann, Nancy, Karen, Maria and Alicia.
3. Rotate the role-play six times so that each individual in the group has the opportunity to play the role of the teacher, bully, bystander, and victim.

4. Tape record each role-played session and play it back to hear how you dealt with this situation when you took on the role of teacher.

DISCUSSION POINTS

Discuss the following points with the entire class:

1. As the teacher, were you able to effectively deal with this situation?
2. What strengths did you bring to the role of teacher?
3. What would you have done differently?
4. How did group members perceive your intervention?
5. What was most challenging for you in the role of teacher?
6. What could the teacher have done to prevent the escalation to violence that occurred during study hall?

NOTEBOOK SECTION FOR CHAPTER 10

BULLYING IN SCHOOLS

I. CONCEPTS/THEORIES

_____

_____

_____

_____

_____

_____

_____

_____

_____

_____

_____

_____

_____

_____

_____

_____

_____

_____

_____

_____

_____

_____

_____

II. CLASSROOM OBJECTIVES

III. BEST PRACTICES (HOW TO IMPLEMENT THOSE OBJECTIVES IN THE CLASSROOM)

WEB RESOURCES

- The Committee for Children has a program called *Steps to Respect: A Bullying Prevention Program*. The *Steps to Respect* curriculum teaches adults how to effectively deal with bullying. Children also learn how to engage in healthy relationships that decrease bullying behavior. The link is:
  http://www.cfchildren.org/strf/strf/strindex
- The United States Substance Abuse and Mental Health Services Administration (SAMHSA) has an initiative called *Make Time to Listen, Take Time to Talk About Bullying*. The program Website features publications such as "Take Action Against Bullying" and "Bullying is Not a Fact of Life." Related links are provided that connect you to the parent education program entitled "Can We Talk?" and the "Olweus Bullying Prevention Program." The link for the Web page is:
  http://www.mentalhealth.samhsa.gov/15plus/aboutbullying.asp
- Bullying.org is a Website that actively supports organizations and individuals who work to end bullying. The Website features information on critical bullying themes such as "You Are Not Alone!" "It's Not Your Fault," and "You Can Do Something About It!" The link to this site is:
  http://www.bullying.org/public/main.cfm?content=0

REFERENCES

American Psychological Association (1999, August 20). *Bullying is not limited to unpopular loners, says researchers; Many children bully each other especially in middle school.* Washington, DC: American Psychological Association. Retrieved June 30, 2005, from http://www.apa.org/releases/bullying.html

Banks, R. (1997). *Bullying in schools.* Champaign, IL: ERIC Clearinghouse on Elementary and Early Childhood Education. (ERIC Document Reproduction Service No. ED407154)

Mestel, R., & Groves, M. (2001, April 3). When push comes to shove. *Los Angeles Times*, pp. E1, E3.

Oliver, R., Hoover, J. H., & Hazler, R. (1994). The perceived roles of bullying in small-town midwestern schools. *Journal of Counseling and Development, 72 (*4), 416-419.

The British Broadcasting Corporation News (1998). *Teachers bully gay pupils.* Retrieved October 23, 2002, from http://news.bbc.co.uk/1/hi/uk/187821.stm

Twemlow, S.W., & Sacco, F.C. (2002). *Some questions parents ask about school bullies.* Retrieved October 23, 2002, from http://www.backoffbully.com/parenttips.html

United States Department of Health and Human Services. (2003). *Bullying is not a fact of life.* Washington, DC: U.S. Department of Health and Human Services.

Vail, K. (1999). Words that wound. *American School Board Journal, 186* (9), 37-40.

Chapter 11

Creating Community through Classroom Management

Creating a classroom environment that promotes learning and awareness is a critical skill for teachers. Academic climate and teacher effectiveness facilitate behaviors conducive to learning (Winzer & Grigg, 1992). Teacher expectations also have an impact on student performance.

Harvard University professor Robert Rosenthal explored whether teacher expectations influence student success. His experiment was conducted with teachers and students at an elementary school (Rosenthal, 1976). Teachers were told that some of the students in the classroom were academically "special." Other students in the class were not given the same positive evaluation, even though there was no actual difference between the two groups. By the end of the academic year, teachers said the "special" children performed better than the other students.

The Rosenthal study highlights the power that teachers have in the classroom. Instructional success for all students means that teachers negotiate classroom communities so that everyone is considered "special." Behavioral management is part of this negotiation. Being able to effectively manage the many behaviors presented in class is imperative for effective teaching and instructional learning (Proctor, 1997).

Classroom management does not mean the same thing as classroom discipline. Classroom management goes beyond just focusing on disciplinary actions. It concerns the broader scope of educational practice and encompasses academic environment, teaching strategies, and the overall structure of the class. Classroom structure includes variables like room arrangement, classroom sounds, teacher location, teacher voice, communication towards students, the nature of class discussions, and classroom tasks (Kohn, 1996). How these variables are managed influences student behavior and sense of connection with the class. Ultimately, the goal of classroom management is to create a community that maximizes the learning potential of all students.

Although discipline is only one component of classroom management, it is significant in the sense that if the teacher cannot effectively manage behavioral problems, everyone's learning suffers. How often have you been in class with a student who dominates class discussions or engages in side bar conversations that make it difficult to listen? Is this student so intent on trying to confuse the teacher that it is hard to stay focused?

These scenarios do three things. First, they interfere with your ability to learn the material. A teacher unable to control inappropriate classroom behavior makes students feel uncomfortable and embarrassed. If you're feeling embarrassed, chances are you aren't focusing on the material being presented. Second, teacher credibility is questioned. If the teacher can't manage the class, how well does he really know the material? Finally, poor classroom management wears a teacher down. Enthusiastic and excited at the beginning of the year, ongoing behavioral problems lead to burnout, frustration, disengagement, and the downward spiral of positive relationships. Wasicsko and Ross (1994) present eight factors that promote effective classroom discipline. These factors are discussed below.

Have high expectations for students. The Rosenthal effect clearly illustrates the importance of positive regard for all students. Having high expectations for students garners their respect, cooperation, and willingness to do well. The bottom line? If you take your students seriously, they will take themselves seriously.

Set classroom parameters. In *Diversity Training Activity 1.2, Setting Classroom Ground Rules,* you and your classmates developed the rules for the course. If students make the rules, they are likely to own and support them. What occurs in class during the first few weeks of school sets the tone for how things will flow the rest of the school year. It is important to set classroom parameters at the beginning of the semester.

Make the implicit explicit. This means that you make your expectations known. Saying, "Don't act out in class" fails to clearly articulate your expectations for behavior. Saying, "Don't talk during study hour" explicitly presents how you expect your students to behave.

Rewards, yes--punishment, no. A teacher who uses excessive punishment is a teacher who is out of control. Punishment is not an effective way to cultivate appropriate classroom behavior. Rewarding positive behavior motivates students to do well, provides a model, and fosters a positive, healthy class environment--not one governed by fear.

Let the punishment fit the crime. The student who acts out in class should be the only student responsible for her behavior (Wasicsko & Ross, 1994). Don't be the frustrated teacher who makes the entire class stay after school because one or two students misbehaved. Not only is punishing everyone unfair, it risks alienating those students who have done well.

Having everyone suffer the same consequences actually invites additional behavioral problems. Students who initially follow the rules decide they aren't going to bother anymore because they still get punished for their peers' bad behavior. Letting the punishment fit the crime means that you are thoughtful about who acts out in class.

Change behavior by removing privileges. This is for the teacher who can't figure out what the consequences for negative behavior should be. When faced with this dilemma, removing privileges is a viable alternative. This strategy changes behavior as it helps the student recognize the direct consequences of his or her actions. Remove privileges soon after the negative behavior occurs so that the connection between negative behavior and consequence is reinforced. Waiting too long to remove the privilege blurs the connection between behavior and consequence. It defeats the learning that can occur when privileges are removed in a timely manner.

Consistency, consistency, consistency. Consistency is a critical part of effective classroom management. Teachers must be clear about rules and classroom expectations. Clarity helps students understand what is expected from them. Inconsistency creates problems (Wasicsko & Ross, 1994). Consider the following scenario:

The teacher tells the class that no make-up exam will be offered for students who don't show up for the final. The only exception is if a student has an emergency. Students must attend class the day of the final and take the exam. Despite the teacher's clarity, two students do not show up the day the exam is given. Two days later they tell the teacher that they overslept and ask to take a make-up exam.

If the teacher lets the students take a make-up, he sends the message that it is acceptable to sleep in late and not take coursework seriously. The students who took the final on time will learn about what happened and not take the teacher seriously the next time he tries to enforce a due date. The end result? Inconsistency threatens teacher credibility.

Know your students. Know your students well enough to know what they think is a punishment and what they consider a reward. One example is the student sent to the hallway for poor classroom behavior. Perhaps this student enjoys being out of class. He sees the "punishment" as a reward (Wasicsko & Ross, 1994). Knowing your students means that you are familiar with their likes and dislikes.

DIVERSITY TRAINING ACTIVITY 11.1
MANAGING CRITICAL CLASSROOM INCIDENTS

RATIONALE

Many first year teachers struggle with how they want to manage their class. Some will come off as too strict to mask the lack of authority they feel. Others will be too lenient in their approach. As you work to find a balance between your style and classroom demands, think about how you will manage particular behavioral incidents.

Drs. France Boutin and Chris Chinien (n.d.) have developed an interactive Website designed to develop classroom management skills and boost first-year teacher confidence in the process. Boutin and Chinien (n.d.) talked to elementary teachers to identify the management issues they struggle with in class. Teachers told them that the main problems they deal with are students who don't perform tasks, disturb classroom activities, are inattentive, don't abide by the rules, show up late for class, refuse to follow instructions, engage in violent behaviors, procrastinate, aren't ready for the school work they are given, have difficulty performing housekeeping tasks, or aren't interested in completing assignments.

Boutin and Chinien (n.d.) made each of these problems a category on their Website. Each category includes a list of critical incidents by grade level that illustrate each particular problem. For instance, an incident in the Failure to Perform Task category is a second grader who does nothing when assigned written work. Your task is to analyze the situation, decide how to respond, compare your response with that of an experienced teacher, and reflect upon your decision to manage the situation. Reflections from actual teachers are also provided where teachers discuss their response to the incidents presented in each category.

STEPS TO IMPLEMENTATION

1. Log in to the Website at http://home.cc.umanitoba.ca/~fboutin/ and click on the book image above the heading entitled *Web-Based Interactive Teacher Development in Classroom Management*.
2. Your instructor will indicate the categories of incidents and corresponding grade levels that you will complete. This *Diversity Training Activity* can be conducted as an in-class or out-of-class assignment, depending upon the availability of computers in your classroom.

3. Go through the step-by-step process of reading and analyzing how you will respond to the specific incidents you are asked to review. Indicate what you will do, look at how an experienced teacher dealt with the situation, consider whether you made the right decision, and read the experienced teachers' rationale for making his or her decision.
4. Print out your response for each critical incident and bring it to class for discussion.

DISCUSSION POINTS

As you review your critical incident responses with the entire class consider the following:

1. Were there categories that you found particularly difficult to deal with?
2. What made it difficult for you to deal with the content and themes raised in these categories?
3. What did you learn from the reflective component of the activity?
4. Were there discrepancies between your approach and the experienced teacher's when it came to managing critical incidents? How did you understand these differences?
5. What did these discrepancies suggest about how you will handle these types of situations in the future?

DIVERSITY TRAINING ACTIVITY 11.2
EIGHT CHALLENGING CLASSROOM BEHAVIORS

RATIONALE

The purpose of *Diversity Training Activity 11.2* is to develop and test your ability to respond to various classroom behavioral problems. *Eight Challenging Classroom Behaviors* will familiarize you with common classroom management issues and suggest useful strategies to cope with them. The role-play component of this activity will involve the entire class, hence you will learn firsthand how these issues play out in a classroom setting.

STEPS TO IMPLEMENTATION

1. Review Table 11.1 to become familiar with eight common behavioral problems. Each problem is presented with a list of strategies designed to help you manage the behavior. Consider these strategies your repertoire of behavioral management interventions.
2. Each student will select at least one behavioral problem that he or she must subsequently "manage" for the class. You will then role-play a teacher in the midst of teaching a subject (choose any topic you like). Your peers will role-play the students in the class who are plagued by the behavioral issue. For instance, when Behavior 1. Talking While You Are Teaching is selected, your peers will role-play students who talk inappropriately during class. They will talk incessantly while you the teacher try to manage their talkative behavior.
3. Make sure that each of the eight challenging classroom behaviors is role-played at least once.
4. Make sure that everyone has a chance to role-play the teacher who tries to manage the challenging behavior.

DISCUSSION POINTS

1. What did you learn about the importance of classroom management through this exercise?
2. What did you learn about your ability to effectively manage a classroom?
3. How do you describe your behavioral management style?
4. What was the most challenging part of this task?
5. How will you deal with the issue you managed in a real classroom setting?

Table 11.1 Eight Challenging Classroom Behaviors

Challenging Behavior	Strategic Response
Behavior 1. Talking While You Are Teaching	• Don't single out the students who are talking. • Move towards them. • Call on them to share their opinions about the lesson. • If necessary, talk with them privately after class.
Behavior 2. Angry Behavior Directed Towards You	• Try not to react in front of the class. • Acknowledge the comment and take it to a class level, asking if others feel the same way. • Rephrase the comment and ask the class their opinion. For instance, "So you think the homework assignment is stupid, how do others feel about this?" • Recognize there may be a larger issue going on for the student such as family problems or academic pressure. • Talk to the student in a calm way after class to determine what is going on.
Behavior 3. Lack of Participation	• Be sensitive about not embarrassing the shy student as you try to encourage participation. • Give the student a leadership role such as being responsible to report small group work to the larger class. • Praise the student for comments made in class. • Make all participants responsible for presenting at least one aspect of a group assignment.
Behavior 4. Dominating Class Time With Extensive Participation	• Acknowledge the student's comment and quickly move away from it. One possible response is: "That's an interesting idea, what do others think?" • Set limits and move on when needed. One possible response is: "I hear your comment, now we need to move on." • Elicit participation from other students. One possible response is: "I'd like to hear from those of you who haven't shared your opinions yet today." • If necessary, talk with the student privately to set limits and determine what is going on.
Behavior 5. Inattentiveness	• Break down assignments into smaller tasks. • Have the student complete a daily progress report that spells out her accomplishments. • Have the student sit at the front of the room to avoid additional distractions that can arise without your proximity. • Refer the student for evaluation if you suspect an attention problem (See Chapter 15. *Exceptional Microcultures: How to Make A Referral*). • Do not lose your patience. • Do not publicly embarrass the student.

Table 11.1 (continued) Eight Challenging Classroom Behaviors

Behavior 6. Complaining in Class	• Do not get defensive. • Hear the student's point. • If appropriate, show your understanding about the difficulty presented. • Depending upon the complaint at hand, ask others if they feel the same way or move on to your lesson plan. • Tell the student you can talk with him privately. One possible response is: "I hear what you're saying. We need to continue with the lesson plan so let's talk during the break."
Behavior 7. Not Taking Responsibility for Classwork	• Keep to your agenda and set appropriate limits. One example involves the student who is late for class and asks you to re-explain the format for the final exam. Your response can be, "We need to continue with the lesson but you can ask one of your classmates for the information." • Set clear parameters for grading such as stating late papers will not be accepted. • Talk about the importance of class participation and attendance. • Build participation and attendance into your grading system.
Behavior 8. Challenging You in Class	• Do not get defensive in front of the class. • Recognize that it is fine not to know everything. If you do not have the answer to a question, one possible response is: "That's an interesting question, how would others respond to that?" or "I'm not certain about the answer to that question but I will look it up and get back to you." • Do not acknowledge the behavior and move on.

NOTEBOOK SECTION FOR CHAPTER 11

CREATING COMMUNITY THROUGH CLASSROOM MANAGEMENT

I. CONCEPTS/THEORIES

_____

_____

_____

_____

_____

_____

_____

_____

_____

_____

_____

_____

_____

_____

_____

_____

_____

_____

_____

_____

_____

_____

_____

II. CLASSROOM OBJECTIVES

III. BEST PRACTICES (HOW TO IMPLEMENT THOSE OBJECTIVES IN THE CLASSROOM)

WEB RESOURCES

- iloveteaching.com addresses issues faced by new, veteran, pre-service, and student teachers. One of the subcategories listed on their homepage specifically deals with classroom management. Subheadings address the first day of school, discipline, and classroom organization. The first day of school Web page, for instance, talks about common mistakes made by first time teachers such as forgetting to set ground rules and expectations during the first week of class. The Web page on discipline discusses discipline related issues such as the boundary between being a teacher and being a friend. Finally, the miscellaneous classroom management and organization Web page suggests how to make your classroom more manageable. Topics include the use of idea cards, how to handle attendance, and dealing with absentee make-up work. The link for the Website is:
  http://www.iloveteaching.com/
- The National Education Association (NEA) has a Web page devoted to classroom management. The Web page reviews techniques used by educators to create a balance between freedom and discipline in the classroom. Techniques are provided for dealing with specific challenges such as attendance, behavior control, prevention, staying ahead, and inclusion. The link for the Website is:
  http://www.nea.org/tips/manage/index.html

REFERENCES

Boutin, F., & Chinien, C. (n.d.). *Classroom management.* Retrieved April 25, 2005, from
    http://home.cc.umanitoba.ca/~fboutin/
Kohn, A. (1996). What to look for in a classroom. *Educational Leadership, 54*(1), 54-55.
Proctor, W., Jr. (1997). A midyear takeover: How to survive. *Teaching Pre K-8, 27*(5), 60-61.
Rosenthal, R. (1976). *Experimenter effects in behavioral research: Enlarged edition.* New
    York: Irvington Publishers.
Wasicsko, M.M., & Ross, S. M. (1994). How to create discipline problems. *The Clearing
    House, 67*(5). 248-252.
Winzer, M., & Grigg, N. (1992). *Educational psychology in the Canadian classroom.*
    Scarborough, ON: Prentice-Hall Canada, Inc.

Chapter 12
Child Abuse and Resilience

Child Abuse: A Problem of National Scope

Child abuse is a problem of national scope with far reaching consequences. According to the U.S. Department of Health and Human Services Administration for Children and Families (n.d.), 1,800,000 referrals alleging child abuse and neglect were reported to child protective services (CPS) in 2002. 896,000 of these reports reflected abuse. 60% of the reports indicated neglect by parents and/or caregivers, 20% involved physical abuse, 10% involved sexual abuse, and 7% involved emotional maltreatment. Almost 20% of the reports were associated with other types of maltreatment (i.e., the fact that a child can experience more than one type of abuse).

More than 80% of the perpetrators of abuse and neglect were parents, 7% were other relatives, and 3% were unmarried partners. The rest were people with other roles (i.e., school personnel) or those whose relationship was unknown. Educators made 16.1% of all reports of abuse and neglect to CPS agencies (U.S. Department of Health and Human Services Administration for Children and Families, n.d.).

Younger children are most at risk for abuse. Children from the ages of 0 to 3 have the highest rates of abuse. 16 out of every 1,000 children within this age range are abused, with girls being more maltreated than boys. In 2002, 1,400 children died from child abuse or neglect. Of these fatalities, 75% involved children who were under 4 years of age, 12% were children between the ages of 4 to 7, 6% between 8 and 11 years of age, and 6% between 12 to 17 years of age.

Infant boys under the age of 1 have the highest fatality rates. 19 out of 100,000 boys and 12 out of 100,000 girls under age 1 die from abuse. Neglect, physical, and sexual abuse all contribute to these deaths (U.S. Department of Health and Human Services Administration for Children and Families, n.d.).

The definition of abuse involves defining different types of maltreatment. Complete *Diversity Training Activity 12.1, Understanding Different Types of Abuse,* at this point in your reading. This activity will help you explore the full meaning of the term child abuse. Through this exercise you will learn what is meant by physical abuse, sexual abuse, neglect, and emotional and psychological abuse. Although these broad categories of abuse exist, to date there is little consensus about how to define abuse. Conceptual differences about how to define abuse make it difficult to prove and document its existence. As a result, it is likely that the prevalence of abuse is underreported and much higher than indicated.

As a mandated reporter, your job is to report the indicators of abuse that you observe (See Mandated Reporting, this chapter). To perform this task it is critical that you are familiar with the general definitions and warning signs associated with the different types of abuse. Under the law, an abused child is a child under the age of 18 whose "parent or other person legally responsible for the child's care inflicts or allows to be inflicted upon the child physical injury by other than accidental means which causes or creates substantial risk of death or serious disfigurement, or impairment of physical health, or loss or impairment of the function of any bodily organ. It is also considered abuse if such a caretaker creates or allows to be created situations whereby a child is likely to be in risk of the dangers mentioned above" (Safe Child Program, n.d.).

Physical abuse of children is abusive behavior that involves physical maltreatment of a child by a caretaker. Physical abuse is indicated by bite marks, unusual bruises, burns, lacerations, frequent injuries or "accidents," fractures in unusual places, discoloration of the skin, beatings, shaking, strangulation, brain damage, and swelling to the face and extremities (Safe Child Program, n.d.).

Sexual abuse is "any sexual contact with a child or the use of a child for the sexual pleasure of someone else" (Safe Child Program, n.d.). Sexual abuse is perhaps one of the most taboo forms of abuse. As such, it is often underreported. It is important to consider sexual abuse on a continuum of behaviors. We tend to think of sexual abuse as involving sexual intercourse but this is only one type of sexually abusive behavior. Other behaviors include fondling of the genitals or asking the child to fondle the genital area, exposing private parts to the child, asking a child to expose him or herself, attempts to enter the vagina or anus with fingers or objects, pornography, prostitution, and voyeurism.

Neglect of children is broadly defined as behaviors by a caregiver that do not provide the child with the basic care necessary for adequate growth and development (Safe Child Program, n.d.). Neglect can include not providing medical care, mental health services, food, shelter, and education. Neglect also occurs when the caregiver does not provide the child with adequate supervision and proper safety. This includes situations where the caregiver is under the influence of alcohol or drugs that lead to impaired judgment and inadequate supervision.

Emotional and psychological abuse of children refers to any abuse that attempts to decrease the child's self-esteem and/or attempts to inflict fear through intimidation. Emotional/psychological abuse is directly aimed at undermining the child's emotional development (Safe Child Program, n.d.). Emotional/psychological abuse includes aggressive, unrealistic demands on the child in the form of impractical expectations and pressure, putting the child down and continually attacking feelings of self-worth. Not following through with verbal promises is another aspect of emotional abuse that fosters disappointment, a lack of trust, and interferes with the ability to develop a healthy dependence.

Physical, Observable, and Behavioral Indicators of the Different Forms of Child Abuse

Research has amply documented the extensive negative effects of child abuse and neglect. These abuses can have physical, psychological, and behavioral consequences that extend over a lifetime. Abusive behaviors can repeat themselves when children who are abused become parents who mistreat their children.

Physical abuse. Physical consequences of child abuse include altered brain development in infancy and early childhood, poor physical health, and long-term health problems such as heart disease, cancer, lung disease, sexually transmitted disease, liver disease, and skeletal fractures (Felitti et al., 1998; Hart, Gunnar, & Cicchetti, 1996). Problems like shaken baby syndrome where the infant is shaken too hard can result in blindness, mental retardation, cerebral palsy, learning disabilities, or paralysis (Conway, 1998).

Behavioral indicators of physical abuse include a child who has no contact with others, suffers from poor self-image, and is unable to trust or love. The child may demonstrate aggressive behavior, display rage, be self-destructive, or engage in passive behavior (Safe Child Program, n.d.). The child may fear entering new relationships or activities. In addition, the child may become apprehensive when other children cry, wear clothing that hides injuries, be secretive and offer inconsistent information about injuries, refuse to undress for gym or for a medical examination for fear that the injury will be exposed, give inconsistent information about how injuries occurred, be afraid of his parents, have frequent absences from school, report abuse by parents, run away from home, be withdrawn, and complain of body aches (Safe Child Program, n.d.). Adolescents may have problems at school, suffer from depression, and experience flashbacks or nightmares similar to symptoms associated with posttraumatic stress disorder (PTSD). They may abuse drugs or alcohol.

Sexual abuse. Physical indicators of sexual abuse include trouble walking or sitting, torn clothing, stained or bloody underwear, pain or itching in the genital area, venereal disease, and pregnancy (Safe Child Program, n.d.). Behavioral indicators of sexual abuse include the child who has either an unusual interest in or an avoidance of things of a sexual nature. The child may experience symptoms of post-traumatic stress, engage in seductive behavior, suffer from depression, feel that one's body is dirty or damaged, refuse to go to school, experience decreased self-esteem, exhibit feelings of worthlessness, display an abnormal or distorted view of self, and be suicidal (Safe Child Program, n.d.).

Youth who have experienced sexual abuse may be very secretive, indicate sexual molestation in drawings, engage in delinquent conduct, and be unusually aggressive. The child may demonstrate a sudden hesitancy to go someplace with someone, act out sexually, use new sexual terms, refuse usual family affection, demonstrate regressive behaviors such as thumb sucking or bedwetting, show signs of fearfulness, clinginess, and changes in personality (Safe Child Program, n.d.).

Neglect. Indicators of neglect vary according to the child's developmental stage. In the very early years, neglected infants and toddlers may be unresponsive to their surroundings. They may not exhibit behaviors that are generally expected for their developmental stage such as smiling, laughing, crying, and reacting to others in general. Neglected infants and toddlers are often not curious about their world. Neglected toddlers may engage in behaviors that reflect earlier stages of development such as rocking or sucking their thumbs.

Some children are hospitalized for failure to thrive (FTT). Infants and toddlers develop this problem when they don't take in an appropriate amount of nutrition. As a result, the FTT child does not grow as expected for his developmental level. There are many cases of children with FTT who have been hospitalized after spending time in a neglectful home environment where the child does not gain the appropriate amount of weight.

Wearing clothing inappropriate for the climate is an observable indicator of neglect. One example is the child who wears summer clothes in winter (Safe Child Program, n.d.). Other observable indicators include being unwashed and wearing dirty clothing. Neglected children often cry easily, even when they are not severely hurt. They may view themselves as failures and appear to be in their own world. Neglected children may be left alone for long periods of time without any supervision. Lack of ongoing supervision is one of the common causes of death among children.

There are also health indicators of neglect. Children who are always tired or complain of physical symptoms are one example. These children may have untreated medical problems such as not getting glasses or desperately needing dental care.

Malnourishment is another health indicator. Malnourished children gorge on food in quick, large gulps, experience frequent hunger, and may look through garbage cans for something to eat. Indicators of neglect are also evident in the school environment. Neglected children may not have lunch money or come to school without a prepared lunch. Children may arrive to school early and say they do not want to go home. Alternatively, children may often be late or absent from school.

Emotional and psychological abuse. Observable indicators of emotional and psychological abuse include regressive behavior such as rocking, sucking, and biting oneself (Safe Child Program, n.d.). The child who experiences emotional abuse may be extremely aggressive, treat others poorly, and restrict play activities. This child may suffer from sleep problems, difficulties with speech, compulsions, and phobias.

Behavioral indicators of emotional abuse include the child who constantly puts himself down. He may be passive and compliant--willing to please others for attention. Emotional abuse can also cause delays in intellectual and emotional development.

Long-term consequences. Psychological consequences of abuse and neglect can last a lifetime. Depression, anxiety, and suicide attempts are serious problems that can result from abuse or neglect (Silverman, Reinherz, & Giaconia, 1996). The insecure early attachment to parents that occurs in an abusive, neglectful environment can lead to relationship problems with peers during adolescence and as an adult (Morrison, Frank, Holland, & Kates, 1999). One study found that 33% of maltreated children grow up to abuse or neglect their children, thus continuing the cycle of abuse (Prevent Child Abuse New York, 2003).

Mandated Reporting

All states and the District of Columbia have mandatory child abuse and neglect reporting laws under the Child Abuse Prevention and Treatment Act (CAPTA). Each state has a listing of professionals and organizations that are required to report child abuse and neglect. Mandated reporters include all types of mental health care providers, teachers, school personnel, social workers, all types of health care providers, daycare providers, and law enforcement personnel. Many states mandate that film developers report child pornography practices. Some states require that all citizens report abuse and neglect.

If you suspect that a child in your school or classroom is being abused or neglected, the first step is to talk with your supervisor or school principal. The school should have policies in place to deal with reporting. Some institutions, for instance, discuss suspected incidences of abuse in a team meeting and have a designated individual call CPS. The CPS agency in the state where the abuse occurs is the service that should be contacted. States, not the federal government, have jurisdiction over matters of child abuse and neglect. Each state has specific laws and procedures for investigation and assessment.

Resilience

Much research exists on the prevention of child abuse and neglect (DiScala, Sege, Guohua, & Reece, 2000; Hwang, 1999; Newberger & Gremy, 2004). While a detailed discussion about prevention efforts are beyond the scope of this chapter, you are encouraged to seek out additional sources about the science of prevention. Resilience is one area of prevention discussed here as it is increasingly viewed as a health promotion intervention strategy.

Resilience has been defined as "the ability to thrive, mature, and increase competence in the face of adverse circumstances or obstacles" (Gordon, 1996, p. 63). It has also been viewed as a "process, capacity or outcome of successful adaptation despite challenges or threatening circumstances...good outcomes despite high risk status, sustained competence under threat and recovery from trauma" (Masten, Best, & Garmezy, 1990, p. 426). Given the prevalence of child abuse, resilience is critical for coping as it means children are better able to deal with life circumstances. Better coping is preventive in the sense that children with resilience resources are better equipped to avoid the development of future problems (Kumpfer, 1999).

Much of the traditional resilience research has focused on individual traits or characteristics that contribute to resilience. These traits include easy temperament, secure attachment, basic trust, problem solving abilities, an internal locus of control, an active coping style, enlisting people to help, making friends, acquiring language and reading well, realistic self-esteem, a sense of harmony, a desire to contribute to others, and faith that one's life matters (Davis, 2001).

While this helps us understand individual aspects of resilience, recent research is moving away from this trait-based approach to look at the role of context in positive outcomes for children. Cultural resilience is "a term that considers those aspects of one's cultural background such as cultural values, norms, supports, language, and customs that promote resilience for individuals and communities. Because culture is all around us, because children operate within different cultural mindsets, and because there are inherent values built into these frameworks, we can no longer talk about resilience without incorporating culture and diversity" (Clauss-Ehlers, 2004, p. 36). Resilience as it is defined and practiced must be relevant to a wide spectrum of culturally diverse youth.

The culturally-focused resilient adaptation (CRA) model asserts that culture and sociocultural context influence resilient adaptation (Clauss-Ehlers, 2004). This means that it is important for you to consider not only your student's individual character traits, but also how culture and environment promote resilience. "Culturally-focused resilient adaptation in the face of adversity is defined as a dynamic, interactive process in which the individual negotiates stress through a combination of character traits, cultural background, cultural values, and facilitating factors in the sociocultural environment" (Clauss-Ehlers, 2004, p. 36). *Diversity Training Activity 12.3, Building Resilience Across Communities of Youth,* is designed to help you understand how resilience processes incorporate culture and diversity.

DIVERSITY TRAINING ACTIVITY 12.1
UNDERSTANDING DIFFERENT TYPES OF ABUSE

RATIONALE

The purpose of *Diversity Training Activity 12.1* is to familiarize you with the different types of abuse. Greater awareness will make you better able to identify warning signs and symptoms associated with abuse and neglect.

STEPS TO IMPLEMENTATION

1. Write out your definition of child abuse. Include a listing of what you consider to be the different types of child abuse.
2. Your instructor will have participants share their definitions of child abuse.
3. Your instructor will write definitions on the board and begin to differentiate the different types of child abuse.
4. At this point your instructor will formally define the different types of abuse that include: physical abuse, emotional/psychological abuse, sexual abuse, and neglect.

DISCUSSION POINTS

As you review the different types of child abuse, consider the following questions with the class:

1. What is your reaction to the different types of abuse that children experience?
2. What signs and symptoms indicate that a child in your classroom is experiencing one or more of these types of abuse?
3. How will you deal with a situation where you suspect a child in your class is being abused or neglected?

DIVERSITY TRAINING ACTIVITY 12.2
BEING A MANDATED REPORTER

RATIONALE

As an educator you are required by law to report suspected child abuse. This process is difficult as it is fraught with concern for the child and her family, the outcome of the report (i.e., will the child be placed in foster care), and the influence reporting will have on perceptions of being a trustworthy educator. The purpose of *Diversity Training Activity 12.2* is to help you become familiar with the process of mandated reporting. This activity is geared to help you feel less overwhelmed about this responsibility.

STEPS TO IMPLEMENTATION

1. Your instructor will divide the class into small groups of 5 to 6 students.
2. Discuss the issue of mandated reporting in your groups.

DISCUSSION POINTS

Consider the following in your group:

1. What concerns do you have about being a mandated reporter?
2. If you found yourself in a situation that you weren't sure required a report or not, what would you do?
3. How do you view your role as a mandated reporter?

DIVERSITY TRAINING ACTIVITY 12.3
BUILDING RESILIENCE ACROSS COMMUNITIES OF YOUTH

RATIONALE

The approach to resilience that incorporates culture and diversity examines what works for different people (Lopez et al., 2002). By looking at the different supports and protective factors that effectively promote resilience processes, the hope is that you will have greater understanding about what fosters resilience for diverse racial/ethnic youth. This awareness is critical as we think about shifting the paradigm of psychological practice from one traditionally focused on disease to one that promotes health.

STEPS TO IMPLEMENTATION

1. Read chapters 4, 5, 6, and 7 in the book *Community Planning to Foster Resilience in Children* (Clauss-Ehlers & Weist, 2004). Each chapter focuses on a different racial/ethnic group as follows: Chapter 4 *Sacred Spaces: The Role of Context in American Indian Youth Development* (LaFromboise & Medoff, 2004); Chapter 5 *Risk and Resilience in Latino Youth* (Javier & Camacho-Gingerich, 2004); Chapter 6 *Building Strengths in Inner City African-American Children: The Task and Promise of Schools* (LaGrange, 2004); and Chapter 7 *Resilience in the Asian Context* (Wong, 2004).
2. Your instructor will divide the class into four groups and assign a chapter to each.
3. As you review the chapter in your group consider the following:
   a. What are some of the within-group differences for this group of youth?
   b. What are the sociocultural stressors faced by this group of youth?
   c. What coping mechanisms are described for this group of youth?
   d. How do resilience processes play out for this group of youth?
4. Prepare a 20-minute presentation for the class that incorporates your responses to the aforementioned questions and present your presentation to the class.

DISCUSSION POINTS

Consider the following in your discussion:

1. What do the different presentations suggest about cultural aspects of resilience?
2. What similarities and differences exist between the presentations?
3. How will you promote resilience in your classroom?

NOTEBOOK SECTION FOR CHAPTER 12
CHILD ABUSE AND RESILIENCE

I. CONCEPTS/THEORIES

_____

_____

_____

_____

_____

_____

_____

_____

_____

_____

_____

_____

_____

_____

_____

_____

_____

_____

_____

_____

_____

_____

_____

II. CLASSROOM OBJECTIVES

III. BEST PRACTICES (HOW TO IMPLEMENT THOSE OBJECTIVES IN THE CLASSROOM)

WEB RESOURCES

- The Safe Child Program has a Website that describes different types of abuse. The Website talks about the prevention of sexual, emotional, and physical abuse as well as safety around strangers. The link is: http://www.safechild.org/index.htm
- The U.S. Department of Health and Human Services Administration for Children and Families provides statistics on child maltreatment, a list of fact sheets, and information about laws, policies, and child welfare reviews. The link for the Website is: http://www.acf.dhhs.gov/programs/cb/publications/cm02/summary.htm

REFERENCES

Clauss-Ehlers, C.S. (2004). Re-inventing resilience: A model of "culturally-focused resilient adaptation". In C.S. Clauss-Ehlers & M.D. Weist (Eds.), *Community planning to foster resilience in children* (pp.27-41). New York, NY: Kluwer Academic Publishers.

Clauss-Ehlers, C.S., & Weist, M.D. (Eds.). (2004). *Community planning to foster resilience in children.* New York, NY: Kluwer Academic Publishers.

Conway, E.E. (1998). Nonaccidental head injury in infants: The shaken baby syndrome revisited. *Pediatric Annals, 27*(10), 677-690.

Davis, N.J. (2001). *Resilience in childhood and adolescence.* Panel presentation delivered at George Washington University, Media Conference, Washington, DC, April.

DiScala, C., Sege, R., Guohua, L., & Reece, R. (2000). Child abuse and unintentional injuries: A 10-year retrospective. *Archives of Pediatric Adolescent Medicine, 154*, 16-22.

Felitti, V.J., Anda, R.F., Nordenberg, D., Williamson, D.F., Spitz, A.M., Edwards, V., Koss, M.P., & Marks, J.S. (1998). Relationship of childhood abuse and household dysfunction to many of the leading causes of death in adults: The adverse childhood experiences (ACE) study. *American Journal of Preventive Medicine 14*(4), 245-258.

Gordon, K.A. (1996). Resilient Hispanic youths, self-concept and motivational patterns. *Hispanic Journal of Behavioral Sciences, 18*, 63-73.

Hart, J., Gunnar, M., & Cicchetti, D. (1996). Altered neuroendocrine activity in maltreated children related to symptoms of depression. *Development and Psychopathology, 8*, 201-214.

Hwang, M. (1999). JAMA patient page: Protecting our children from child abuse. *Journal of the American Medical Association, 282*, 500.

Javier, R.A., & Camacho-Gingerich, A. (2004). Risk and resilience in Latino youth. In C.S. Clauss-Ehlers & M.D. Weist (Eds.), *Community planning to foster resilience in children* (pp.65-81). New York, NY: Kluwer Academic Publishers.

Kumpfer, K.L. (1999). Factors and processes contributing to resilience: The resilience framework. In M.D. Glantz & J.L. Johnson (Eds.), *Resilience and development: Positive life adaptations* (pp. 179-224). New York, NY: Kluwer Academic/Plenum Publishers.

LaFromboise, T., & Medoff, L. (2004). Sacred spaces: The role of context in American Indian youth development. In C.S. Clauss-Ehlers & M.D. Weist (Eds.), *Community planning to foster resilience in children* (pp.45-63). New York, NY: Kluwer Academic Publishers.

LaGrange, R.D. (2004). Building strengths in inner city African-American children: The task and promise of schools In C.S. Clauss-Ehlers & M.D. Weist (Eds.), *Community planning to foster resilience in children* (pp.83-97). New York, NY: Kluwer Academic Publishers.

Lopez, S.J., Prosser, E.C., Edwards, L.M., Magyar-Moe, J.L., Neufeld, J.E., & Rasmussen, H.N. (2002). Putting positive psychology in a multicultural context. In C.R. Snyder & S.J. Lopez (Eds.), *Handbook of positive psychology* (pp. 700-714). New York: Oxford University Press.

Masten, A.S., Best, K.M., & Garmezy, N. (1990). Resilience and development: Contributions from the study of children who overcome adversity. *Development and Psychopathology, 2*, 425-222.

Morrison, J.A., Frank, S.J., Holland, C.C., & Kates, W.R. (1999). Emotional development and disorders in young children in the child welfare system. In J.A. Silver, B.J. Amster, & T. Haecker (Eds.), *Young children and foster care: A guide for professionals* (pp. 33-64). Baltimore, MD: Paul H. Brookes Publishing Company.

Newberger, C.M., & Gremy, I.M. (2004). Clinical and institutional interventions and children's resilience and recovery from sexual abuse. In C.S. Clauss-Ehlers & M.D. Weist (Eds.), *Community planning to foster resilience in children* (pp.197-215). New York, NY: Kluwer Academic Publishers.

Prevent Child Abuse New York. (2003). *Causes and consequences: The urgent need to prevent child abuse.* Retrieved April 6, 2005, from www.pca-ny.org/pdf/cancost.pdf

Safe Child Program (n.d.). *Safe child: Child abuse.* Retrieved April 6, 2005, from http://www.safechild.org/index.htm

Silverman, A.B., Reinherz, H.Z., & Giaconia, R.M. (1996). The long-term sequelae of child and adolescent abuse: A longitudinal community study. *Child Abuse and Neglect, 20*(8), 709-723.

United States Department of Health and Human Services Administration for Children and Families (n.d.). *Children's bureau: Summary child maltreatment 2002.* Retrieved April 6, 2005, from http://www.acf.dhhs.gov/programs/cb/publications/cm02/summary.htm

Wong, G. (2004). Resilience in the Asian context. In C.S. Clauss-Ehlers & M.D. Weist (Eds.), *Community planning to foster resilience in children* (pp.99-111). New York, NY: Kluwer Academic Publishers.

Section 5

Understanding Exceptional Microcultures

Chapter 13

Exceptional Microcultures: Dealing with Trauma

Trauma was not initially a part of my course curricula when I started to teach the Individual and Cultural Diversity course in September 2001. My students and I were only one week into the course when the terrorist attacks on the World Trade Center and the Pentagon occurred and a plane crashed in Somerset County, Pennsylvania. Then on November 12, 2001, American Airlines flight 587 crashed en route from New York City to the Dominican Republic in Queens, New York.

Given this context, trauma quickly became an integral part of student learning. Discussion about the meaning of trauma, identifying symptoms, and appropriate classroom intervention were particularly relevant as students shared their own exposure to extreme stress. A Middle Eastern student discussed how she went to get gasoline after September 11th and the attendant said he would not sell gas to a terrorist. Another student shared how she sat by the phone feeling helpless as her family waited to hear from her father who worked at the World Trade Center. While they learned of his survival that evening, the student described the stress that stayed with her as a result of dealing with the terrifying unknown.

During the past two decades the effects of trauma among children and adolescents have been more amply studied (Pynoos, Steinberg, & Goenjian, 1996). Pynoos et al. (1996) describe traumatic situations as "the experience of external threat [that] involves an estimation of the extreme magnitude of the threat, the unavailability or ineffectiveness of contemplated or actual protective actions by self or others, and the experience of physical helplessness at irreversible traumatic moments. The experience of internal threat includes a sense of inability to tolerate the affective responses and physiological reactions, as well as a sense of catastrophic personal consequence" (p. 338).

Empirical studies of trauma among children and adolescents underscore its prevalence. Studies have found that 23% of American adolescents experience physical or sexual assault and witness violence against others. Of these, 20% developed post-traumatic stress disorder (PTSD). This means that approximately 1.07 million U.S. teenagers have PTSD (Kilpatrick, Saunders, Resnick, & Smith, 1995).

Six factors highlight the complexity of trauma experienced by children and adolescents (Pynoos et al., 1996). First, the child's affect, cognitive state, and developmental stage must be considered at the time of the traumatic event. Second, it is important to recognize how challenging it will be for the child to manage intense physiological and emotional reactions to the traumatic situation. Third, children may experience different levels of concern and attention associated with the traumatic event. Fourth, an intense change in the child's concern and attention may occur when autonomy and physical integrity are threatened to the point that the child dissociates from the trauma. Fifth, additional aspects of traumatic stress may occur after the immediate threat ends. The child who stays by an injured family member until help arrives is one such example. Sixth, the experience of trauma for children and adolescents is multilayered and can include a buildup of various stressors such as anxiety about the well-being of friends and family members, having to witness the death of an attachment figure, and the current trauma reminding the child of an earlier traumatic situation (Pynoos et al., 1996).

It is important to recognize and understand typical responses to disaster and trauma. Shock and denial are two mechanisms that are part of a normal, protective human reaction to traumatic events. Shock is the sudden, intense disturbance to one's emotional state that leaves the individual feeling dazed and stunned (American Psychiatric Association, 1994). Denial occurs when the individual does not acknowledge that something stressful has happened (American Psychiatric Association, 1994). A child may continue to wait for the return of his father, for instance, despite being told that he died in the World Trade Center. Other responses to trauma are unpredictable feelings, increased irritability, flashbacks, nightmares, fear that the event will re-occur, and problems in interpersonal relationships.

When these difficulties become chronic and ongoing, a child may have PTSD. A child is at greater risk of developing PTSD if the trauma is serious, the trauma gets repeated, and the child is physically close to the trauma. The nature of the child's relationship to the victim is also a determining factor in the development of PTSD (Clauss-Ehlers, Acosta, & Weist, 2004).

The *Diagnostic and Statistical Manual of Mental Disorders* (American Psychiatric Association, 1994) describes three general categories of symptoms associated with PTSD: re-experiencing the trauma, avoiding anything associated with the trauma, and ongoing symptoms of increased arousal not present before the trauma. Re-experiencing the trauma means that some trauma-specific reenactment occurs. For instance, the young child may engage in repetitive play where aspects of the trauma are consistently expressed. A seven-year-old girl who repeatedly draws pictures of planes crashing into the World Trade Center is re-experiencing the traumatic event through her artwork. Other children may have re-occurring nightmares about the trauma they survived.

Avoidance of stimuli linked to the trauma involves efforts to stay clear of those activities, places, and people that remind the individual of the traumatic experience. A mother I saw for psychotherapy after the 1997 Empire State Building shooting illustrates the notion of avoidance. In February 1997 a shooter opened fire on the Empire State Building's observation deck. The shooter killed one person, injured six, and then shot himself in the head. This woman lay on top of her child to protect her while the shooting went on. Both mother and child survived.

In our work together, the mother shared that she couldn't take the subway to attend our sessions. The subway, an enclosed public space like the Empire State Building's observation deck, reminded her of the traumatic incident she and her daughter survived. She associated the subway with being trapped in a dangerous public space.

The individual who cannot recall an important aspect of the trauma is another aspect of avoidance. One example is a woman who escaped the World Trade Center. The woman sought psychotherapy because she was terrified about having absolutely no recollection of climbing down many flights of stairs on September 11th.

Persistent avoidance also takes the form of feeling detached from others. After losing his father on September 11th, for instance, one eleven-year-old boy distanced himself from his mother and younger sister. In therapy the boy eventually shared that he was afraid to be close to surviving family members in the event that they too would not return home one day.

Having a sense of a foreshortened future is another way that individuals avoid trauma-related stimuli. I was a panelist on a call-in television news show that aired soon after September 11th. A grandmother called the station to talk about her grandson's emotional state. She was sad and confused about what he had recently told her. Amidst all the talk about September 11th, her grandson said, "What's it all matter? We're all going to die anyway."

Having ongoing symptoms of increased arousal not present before the trauma means the individual experiences greater vigilance after the trauma. Increased arousal means your body works overtime to protect itself from potential danger. This overprotection manifests itself through changes like difficulty falling or staying asleep, irritability, difficulty concentrating, hypervigilance, and having an exaggerated startle response (American Psychiatric Association, 1994). One example is the child who slept well before a traumatic event but now lies awake with the light on at all times.

Cultural Aspects of Trauma

Culture influences how people interpret traumatic events (Clauss-Ehlers & Lopez Levi, 2002). A culturally-inclusive response to trauma must consider gender roles, interpretation of the event, stigma, and religious persecution (See Clauss-Ehlers et al., 2004). It is important that services assess their effectiveness. The following example illustrates how outreach must be sensitive to the particular needs of the diverse populations they are designed to serve:

> Faced with the aftermath of September 11th, many organizations set up booths to provide various services. Due to the lock down state of New York City at that time, a police presence was in view of many of these service outlets. Unfortunately, the police presence acted as a deterrent to seeking services for many individuals and families from culturally diverse communities. Having escaped torture, come to the US for political refuge, or been victimized in their countries of origin, the police presence acted as an unintentional re-traumatization for many. It is a difficult position to try to balance security versus services during a time of crisis. A possible alternative might be to provide access to some services separate and apart from law enforcement, or if this is not appropriate, for security personnel to be dressed less formally (Clauss-Ehlers et al., 2004, pp. 151-152).

Additional issues to consider if trauma-intervention efforts are to be culturally-sensitive include a mistrust of government authorities, language barriers, and religious background.

Lack of access to benefits also has implications for culturally-relevant treatment. When I first started to work with Spanish-speaking families who lost a loved one on September 11th, for instance, the mental health contract only allowed for three sessions. To connect with a grieving family and stop counseling after only three sessions directly contradicts the Latino cultural value of *personalismo* where the relationship is of utmost importance (Clauss-Ehlers & Lopez Levi, 2002).

For a family to openly share their grief and end therapy after three weeks also flies in the face of effective trauma relief efforts. Ending grief work so abruptly and without any closure risks re-traumatizing the family as they confront the loss of the therapist and their grief remains raw. Table 13.1 provides a listing of culturally-inclusive responses to trauma and examines cultural framework, practical problems, and specific cross-cultural interventions.

Table 13.1 Culturally-Inclusive Responses to Trauma

CULTURAL FRAMEWORK	PRACTICAL PROBLEMS	SPECIFIC CROSS-CULTURAL INTERVENTION
Search for the meaning of suffering and pain relevant to the culture	Deal with immediate problems the individual is having difficulty handling	• Ask survivors how you can be of assistance to them and then tell them truthfully what you can and can't do
Search for the meaning of death in the culture	Build trust	• Work to reduce isolation
Search for the meaning of life in the culture	Assist with financial resources if possible	• Provide relaxation techniques/meditation
Traditions may help survivors feel re-oriented	Help survivors focus on something tangible that they can accomplish over the next few days	• Provide education about the crisis in culturally relevant terms • Help the individual develop control • Work with the individual to increase self-esteem and decrease self-blame or survival guilt • Be aware of culturally relevant communication techniques: - Eye contact - Integration of food and drink - Pace of conversation - Body language

Note: Select recommendations are included here. See NASP website for a full listing of their recommendations. Table not a reproduction of any NASP table. Table is based on a table printed in Clauss-Ehlers, C.S., Acosta, O., & Weist, M.D. (2004). Terrorism: Voices of two communities speak out. In C.S. Clauss-Ehlers & M.D. Weist (Eds.), *Community planning to foster resilience in children* (pp.143-159). New York, NY: Kluwer Academic Publishers. Reproduced with permission from Springer.

DIVERSITY TRAINING ACTIVITY 13.1
DEVELOPMENTAL ASPECTS OF TRAUMA

RATIONALE

A child can experience trauma at any age. Signs and symptoms vary among preschoolers and kindergarteners, elementary school children, and adolescents in junior and senior high school. While your job as an educator is not to diagnose a child with a trauma-related disorder, you can identify signs and symptoms that require a referral (See Chapter 15 *Exceptional Microcultures: How to Make a Referral*). The classroom intervention section of this activity gives you tools to use if your classroom is affected by a traumatic incident. The purpose of *Diversity Training Activity 13.1* is to help you feel equipped to deal with crisis situations rather than become paralyzed in the wake of disaster. The information provided below is based on the New York City Board of Education (2001) response to the events of September 11th and provides a true-to-life illustration of educator approach and goals.

STEPS TO IMPLEMENTATION

1. Table 13.2 presents developmental aspects of traumatic signs and symptoms. Your instructor will divide the class into small groups of 5 to 6 students each. Review the information presented in the table as you discuss age-specific traumatic symptoms in your small group.
2. Having reviewed age-related symptoms, discuss potential classroom interventions that you can implement for each age group.
3. Compare the interventions you suggest to those presented in Tables 13.3, 13.4, and 13.5.

DISCUSSION POINTS

Having reviewed symptoms and interventions, the following questions form the focus of class discussion. Share responses with your small groups and then with the entire class. Questions for discussion include:

1. How will you start a conversation about a traumatic event with your students?
2. How will you manage your own reaction to the trauma while trying to process those of your students?
3. What will you do if a student shares that he lost a loved one?
4. What will you do if you notice a student becoming symptomatic several months after the trauma occurred?

Table 13.2 Traumatic Symptoms for Preschoolers, Kindergarteners, Elementary School Students, Junior and Senior High School Students

Developmental Domain	Manifestation of Symptoms for Preschoolers and Kindergarteners	Manifestation of Symptoms for Elementary School Students	Manifestation of Symptoms for Junior and Senior High School Students
Cognitive	• Decreased attention • Confusion about the event such as where it occurred and who was injured or died	• Decreased concentration • Confusion about the event such as where it occurred and who was injured or died	• Decreased concentration • Concern about one's health
Behavioral	• Repetitive play • Regression to an earlier stage of development (i.e., bedwetting) • Nightmares	• Regression to an earlier stage of development • Nightmares • Decrease in school performance • Clinginess • Acting out behavior	• Drug and alcohol abuse • Inability to meet responsibilities • Social isolation • Decrease in school performance • Survival guilt • Aggressive behavior • Regression to prior coping styles • Becoming too old too soon (i.e., dropping out of school to join the work world, pregnancy)
Physical	• Sleep problems • Bladder problems • Eating problems (i.e., not eating or overeating)	• Sleep problems • Psychosomatic complaints (i.e., headaches with no medical problem)	• Eating problems (i.e., not eating or overeating) • Psychosomatic complaints (i.e., headaches with no medical problem)
Emotional	• Feelings of nervousness • Lack of spontaneity • Fear of stimuli that act as reminders of the trauma	• Fear for family safety • Guilt • Fear of school • Fear of trauma repeating itself	• Anxiety • Depression

Note: Table based in part on information from the New York City Department of Education (2001).

Table 13.3 Classroom Interventions for Preschoolers and Kindergarteners

Objectives	Interventions
To re-establish an ongoing routine as quickly as possible.	• Re-establish the routine of daily school activities.
To re-establish a sense of safety as quickly as possible.	• Be prepared to talk with children about the trauma if the topic is raised.
To re-establish a sense of independence and autonomy, an important developmental goal of this age.	• Offer children age appropriate ways to communicate their experience about the trauma through drawings, stories, free play, and discussion. • Offer physical comforts such as nap time, story time, and snack time.

Note: Table based in part on information from the New York City Department of Education (2001).

Table 13.4 Classroom Interventions for Elementary School Students

Objectives	Interventions
To re-establish a sense of safety as quickly as possible.	• Offer children the ongoing opportunity to express their feelings about the event.
To re-establish a sense of productivity, an important developmental goal of this age.	• Re-establish the routine of daily school activities.
To relieve guilt.	• Let children know that their reactions are normal and there is not any one particular way to react.
To enhance self-esteem.	• Be flexible in terms of academic requirements after the trauma. • Reinforce age appropriate behavior.

Note: Table based in part on information from the New York City Department of Education (2001).

Table 13.5 Classroom Interventions for Junior and Senior High School Students

Objectives	Interventions
To provide reassurance of normalcy.	• Offer adolescents the ongoing opportunity to express their feelings about the event.
To re-establish a sense of safety as quickly as possible.	• Offer adolescents the ongoing opportunity to express their fears about the event.
To encourage discussion of feelings of depression and anxiety.	• Validate responses by letting students know there is no one particular way to react to a traumatic event.
To get students back on their life course.	• Help students channel their feelings into proactive activities (i.e., volunteer work). • Be flexible in terms of academic requirements after the trauma. • Talk about risk factors during this time (i.e. substance use, pregnancy). • Provide guidance about the student's life goals and hopes for the future.

Note: Table based in part on information from the New York City Department of Education (2001).

NOTEBOOK SECTION FOR CHAPTER 13
EXCEPTIONAL MICROCULTURES: DEALING WITH TRAUMA

I. CONCEPTS/THEORIES

II. CLASSROOM OBJECTIVES

III. BEST PRACTICES (HOW TO IMPLEMENT THOSE OBJECTIVES IN THE CLASSROOM)

_____

_____

_____

_____

_____

_____

_____

_____

_____

_____

_____

_____

_____

_____

_____

_____

_____

_____

_____

_____

_____

_____

_____

_____

_____

_____

_____

_____

_____

WEB RESOURCES

- The National Child Traumatic Stress Network addresses the standard of care and services for traumatized children, families, and communities. The Website offers resources and networks for parents, caregivers, and school personnel. The link to the Website is:
http://www.nctsnet.org
- The National Center for Post Traumatic Stress Disorder provides information, fact sheets, videos, and links associated with children and adolescents who have been traumatized. The link for the Website is:
http://www.ncptsd.org/topics/children.html

REFERENCES

American Psychiatric Association (1994). *Diagnostic and statistical manual of mental disorders* (4th ed.). Washington, DC: Author.

Clauss-Ehlers, C.S., Acosta, O., & Weist, M.D. (2004). Terrorism: The voices of two communities speak out. In C.S. Clauss-Ehlers & M.D. Weist (Eds.), *Community planning to foster resilience in children* (pp.143-159). New York: Kluwer Academic Publishers.

Clauss-Ehlers, C.S., & Lopez Levi, L. (2002). Working to promote resilience with Latino youth in schools: Perspectives from the U.S. and Mexico. *International Journal of Mental Health Promotion, 4*(4), 14-20.

Kilpatrick, D.G., Saunders, B.E., Resnick, H.S., & Smith, D.W. (1995*). The national survey of adolescents: Preliminary findings on lifetime prevalence of traumatic events and mental health correlates*. Manuscript submitted for publication.

New York City Department of Education (2001). Information on signs and symptoms of trauma in students and classroom interventions. New York, NY: Author.

Pynoos, R.S., Steinberg, A.M., & Goenjian, A. (1996). Traumatic stress in childhood and adolescence: Recent developments and current controversies. In B.A. vanderKolk, A. C. McFarlane, & L. Weisaeth (Eds.), *Traumatic stress: The effects of overwhelming experience on mind, body , and society* (pp. 331-358). New York, NY: The Guilford Press.

Chapter 14

Exceptional Microcultures: Youth with Emotional Disturbance-Childhood Depression, Eating Disorders

Mental health issues have a profound effect on children's well-being and development. A child who suffers from clinical depression, for instance, may become increasingly withdrawn and uninterested in school. Once active and curious, this student is now reclusive and less participatory.

Knowledge is power but when it comes to information about children's mental health, ours is a nation of contrasts. Although books line the shelves of child development sections at popular book retailers, gaps in public knowledge about children's mental health abound. The Pew Littleton Charitable Trust, for instance, found that Columbine was one of the most followed stories of the 1990s simply because people could not fully understand what had occurred (Clauss-Ehlers & Weist, 2002; Gibbs, 1999).

The U.S. Department of Health and Human Services (1998) estimates that 10% of youth have a serious emotional disturbance. Despite this large percentage, 66% of children and adolescents with mental health problems do not get the treatment they need (U.S. Department of Health and Human Services; 1998). The disparity between prevalence and lack of intervention suggests major gaps in public awareness and knowledge about children's mental health. Questions raised by this discrepancy are: Is the lack of response due to the inability to recognize signs and symptoms of mental health problems among our youth? Are children not getting necessary treatment due to inadequate mental health services? Who can children turn to when they experience a mental health problem like depression or anxiety?

The Role of Stigma in Children's Mental Health

Responses to the above questions must be understood within the context of stigma. Stigma is an abstract concept that involves misperceptions of people with mental illnesses. Stigma is characterized by painful, destructive, discriminatory attitudes and behaviors towards those with mental health problems (Clauss-Ehlers & Weist, 2002). The media perpetuates this view by often portraying individuals with mental illnesses as violent, criminal offenders. Stigma also leads people to deny that they are experiencing mental health problems. People don't want to be labeled, so they say they don't have a problem. People with mental illnesses are often blamed for their problems. They are looked at as being unable to "pull themselves up by their boot straps."

Stigma is particularly relevant to children's mental health. Historically some psychologists believed that children didn't have adequately developed ego strength to experience mental health problems (Freud, 1894, 1896). Many believed that infants, children, and adolescents couldn't suffer from depression because they lacked the ego capacity to realize that they were depressed (Clauss-Ehlers & Weist, 2002). The implication of this historical belief is that youth do not need mental health services because they cannot experience mental health problems like depression. Stigma comes in to play when attitudes and belief systems deny children the option of receiving help because of these mistaken assumptions.

Not seeking help for children with mental health problems reflects common myths about childhood in the U.S. As a nation we tend to view childhood as a time of play, free from worry and stress (Clauss-Ehlers & Weist, 2002). When problems develop common responses are "She's just a kid" or "It's just a stage he's going through." People struggle to acknowledge that not all problems children experience are a reflection of where they are at developmentally. Research conducted at Ball State and Columbia University is a case in point. Researchers at these universities found that of the 57% of adolescents who suffered from depression and attempted suicide, only 13% of their parents recognized that their child was depressed (Chua-Eoan, 1999).

The Educator's Role in Children's Mental Health

Educators are physically present in students' lives for a large portion of their day. Many students spend more time with their teachers than their parents. This gives you the educator the unique vantage point of noticing changes in the mood, behavior, academic performance, and social engagement of your students. This does not mean that you have to treat or diagnose the changes you see. These responses go beyond the scope of training. Your ongoing relationship and proximity with students, however, allows for a potentially important role in their well-being as you can call attention to observable changes in attitude and behavior.

Chapter 14 focuses on definitions and warning signs associated with children's mental health. Numerous mental health problems affect youth and an all-encompassing discussion is beyond the scope of this chapter. Instead, you are encouraged to seek out information about the range of issues youth struggle with, especially if one of your students has a particular problem.

Major depressive disorder, anorexia nervosa, and bulimia are the focus of this chapter. These disorders are discussed because of their high prevalence among youth and potential influence on classroom performance. A child who suffers from major depressive disorder, for instance, risks doing poorly at school due to symptoms like decreased concentration, inattentiveness, and irritability.

Child and Adolescent Depression

Diversity Training Activity 14.1 provides an overview of depression among youth. Take a moment and complete the quiz presented in Table 14.1a. Compare your responses to quiz answers that are listed in Table 14.1b. Discussion questions are designed to have your class engage in a dialogue about the consequences of depression among youth.

Depressive disorders include major depressive disorder, bipolar disorder, and dysthymic disorder. Major depressive disorder is a unipolar depression where the individual persistently experiences low mood and sadness. Bipolar disorder, formerly known as manic depression, is characterized by extreme shifts in mood that vacillate between high and low affect. Dysthymic disorder is a chronic, mild depression that can be ongoing over the course of many years. Each type of depression is characterized by specific symptoms. Major depressive disorder is the focus of the discussion below.

Major depressive disorder. Major depressive disorder in youth often goes unrecognized by families and physicians. Major depressive disorder affects up to 2.5% of children and 8.3% of adolescents in the U.S. (Birmaher et al., 1996). Currently there is an earlier onset of depression in comparison to previous decades, meaning that children are becoming depressed at a younger age (Klerman & Weissman, 1989). Being depressed earlier on in life can have a negative influence on interpersonal and developmental experiences that are important for young children to master.

The educator who recognizes the warning signs of depression can better understand why a student acts the way he does. Identification of warning signs, for instance, will help you view Johnny's aggression as a symptom of depression rather than Johnny simply misbehaving again. Several points, however, deserve further clarification. First, having one or two depressive symptoms does not mean a child is clinically depressed. At least five symptoms must be present during most days for a period of two weeks or more to meet diagnostic criteria for major depressive disorder (American Psychiatric Association, 1994). This makes sense since everyone has bad days and may feel sad, tearful, or irritable on occasion. These normal responses to daily life events do not make for a diagnosis.

A second point concerns how hard it is to identify depression in young children. Young children are just learning how to express their feelings. They act them out (i.e., having a tantrum or crying) instead of saying: "I feel

sad because grandpa died" or "I am depressed because I miss my pet."
Misinterpreting behaviors gets in the way of making an accurate diagnosis.
Rather than recognize a child is angry because he is depressed, for instance,
adults may simply think the child is misbehaving. This type of
misinterpretation can lead to punishing the child rather than referring him for
treatment.

A third point is that children have different depressive symptoms than
adults. While some symptoms are shard by children, adolescents, and adults,
others only occur during the younger years. Symptoms common to children,
adolescents, and adults are (American Psychiatric Association, 1994):

- Persistent sad or irritable mood
- Anhedonia (a lack of interest in activities that were once pleasurable)
- Ongoing thoughts of death or dying, including suicide
- Difficulty sustaining attention or concentrating
- Change in eating patterns, i.e., overeating or loss of appetite
- Change in sleeping patterns, i.e., insomnia or hypersomnia
- Decreased energy
- Slowed physical movements
- Feelings of worthlessness

These shared symptoms of depression reflect a commonality of
experience across age groups. Developmental considerations must also be
taken into account, however, and point to the differences between children,
adolescents and adults. Infants and young children who suffer from
depression may appear unresponsive to stimuli in their environment. They
may not have significant attachments or be interpersonally limited. Infants
and very young children who suffer from major depressive disorder may fail
to meet developmental milestones in an age appropriate manner. One
example is the young school-aged child who starts to wet his bed again.

Children and adolescents who suffer from depression may experience a
drop in academic performance and have poor school attendance. Complaints
of headaches and stomachaches to stay home may become routine behavior.
Depressed children and adolescents are likely to feel bored, irritable, cry
often, have difficulty communicating with others, and express a fear of
death. Youth in both age groups are likely to demonstrate a marked change
in relationships with family and friends. They may isolate themselves and
not want to spend time with loved ones.

Depression is linked to substance abuse and suicide in the pre-adolescent
and adolescent years (Birmaher, Brent, & Benson, 1998). Suicide is the third
leading cause of death among 10-to-24-year-olds (Hoyert, Kochanek, &
Murphy, 1999). Warning signs associated with youth suicide are boredom,
physical complaints, withdrawal from friends, feeling like a bad person,

substance use, euphoria after a state of depression, taking care of business (i.e., giving things away), and verbal indicators (i.e., a young person who says "What's the point? Nothing matters anyway."). Depression can be treated with medication and/or psychotherapy.

Eating disorders. Eating disorders almost always begin in adolescence and have emotional and spiritual components. Emotionally, the adolescent uses food as a release from anxiety. Spiritually, food becomes a mechanism for letting go. Families of teenagers with eating disorders may be enmeshed, achievement oriented, and perfectionistic; not value the expression of feelings; and involve the child in parental conflicts (Kog & Vandereycken, 1989).

Anorexia nervosa. Anorexia nervosa is one type of eating disorder. 90% of those with anorexia are girls and 10% are boys. A common misconception is that people with anorexia are afraid of food. The opposite is actually the case. People with anorexia are often obsessed with food--cooking it, reading about it, looking at pictures of it, and being engaged in any food-related behavior as long as it does not involve food consumption. Anorexia is not a fear of food, but a fear of getting fat.

Someone with anorexia nervosa refuses to "maintain a minimally normal body weight, is intensely afraid of gaining weight, and exhibits a significant disturbance in the perception of shape or size of his or her body" (American Psychiatric Association, 1994, p. 539). Even though the individual is dangerously thin, she does not eat because she is afraid she will gain weight. The individual with anorexia tries to maintain control of what, when, and where she consumes her food. One's weight and perception of body shape have an enormous influence on self-esteem and self-evaluation. The individual bases her value on being underweight and evaluates her sense of self according to what she weighs.

Anorexia nervosa takes a physical toll on the body. It involves the absence of at least three consecutive menstrual cycles and can lead to physical problems like having an electrolyte imbalance, hair loss, a drop in blood pressure, fainting, heart failure, low blood sugar, muscle weakness, and decreased concentration (American Psychiatric Association, 1994). These serious physical problems can lead to permanent damage and even death.

Bulimia nervosa. The essential features of bulimia are "binge eating and inappropriate compensatory methods to prevent weight gain" (American Psychiatric Association, 1994, p. 545). Binge eating involves eating an exorbitantly high amount of food in a short period of time. The amount of food ingested is more than normal and the individual feels a loss of control during the binge. A range of foods may be consumed throughout the binge although they tend to be sweet and high in calories (American Psychiatric Association, 1994).

The individual with bulimia often feels ashamed of her eating problems and will go to great lengths to hide them. As a result, binge eating is often done in secret (American Psychiatric Association, 1994). Various stressors can initiate binge eating such as interpersonal problems, low mood, hunger, negative feelings about one's body, and food in general. It is common for the individual to feel depressed after the binge is over (American Psychiatric Association, 1994).

The adolescent engages in inappropriate compensatory behaviors to make up for binge eating. Vomiting is the most common compensatory method that is used after a binge. 80 to 90% of individuals who seek treatment at eating disorder clinics use vomiting as a compensatory measure (American Psychiatric Association, 1994). Other ways that people with bulimia try to offset potential weight gain from binge eating are using diet pills, laxatives, fasting, and extreme exercise. As with anorexia nervosa, the self worth of the person with bulimia nervosa is influenced by perceptions of body image.

Cultural factors associated with eating disorders. A common stereotype is that White, higher socioeconomic, heterosexual adolescent girls are those who develop eating disorders. Of course there are girls with eating disorders who meet this demographic profile, however, these characteristics in no way represent everyone with anorexia nervosa or bulimia. Anorexia nervosa is more "prevalent in industrialized societies, in which there is abundance of food and in which, especially for females, being considered attractive is linked to being thin" (American Psychiatric Association, 1994, p. 542). Eating disorders are most common in the United States, Europe, Australia, Japan, New Zealand, and South Africa although additional epidemiological studies need to be conducted in other cultures (American Psychiatric Association, 1994).

Individuals who immigrate to an industrialized country from a culture where eating disorders aren't prevalent may develop an eating disorder as they acculturate to the new culture's view of body image. Being able to assess the individual's degree of acculturation helps determine how the immigration experience has influenced the development of the eating disorder. Many countries value body fat and consider extra weight a sign of affection and beauty. The term *gordita* used in Latin American cultures, for instance, literally means little fat one. It is considered a sign of affection and endearment. As the individual internalizes the Western notion of a thin-body ideal, however, the value of being a *gordita* gets lost.

Knowledge of signs and symptoms associated with mental health problems enhances your capacity to accurately interpret student behavior. For instance, the child's angry behavior is now understood as the irritability that comes with depression and an indirect cry for help. Similarly, problems with concentration and class participation are accurately perceived as symptoms of depression instead of a lack of interest in coursework. Your proximity to children puts you in the unique position of responding to warning signs that go unrecognized by others. You can talk to school administrators and parents about your observations and start the referral process (see Chapter 15. *Exceptional Microcultures: How to Make a Referral*).

DIVERSITY TRAINING ACTIVITY 14.1
CHILDHOOD DEPRESSION QUIZ

RATIONALE

The purpose of this activity is to assess your knowledge and awareness about the prevalence of depression in children and adolescents.

STEPS TO IMPLEMENTATION

1. Take the quiz below. Review answers with the class (See Table 14.1b).

Table 14.1a Childhood Depression Quiz

Question	Response
1. Children do not have sufficient ego development to suffer from depression.	True False
2. Treatment for childhood depression is usually not successful.	True False
3. Intervention soon after symptoms develop can promote effective treatment and prevent long term problems.	True False
4. Most children and adolescents with mental health problems get treatment.	True False
5. 2% of youth can benefit from some type of mental health intervention.	True False
6. In 1997, suicide was the third leading cause of death among 10-to-24 year-olds.	True False
7. As many as 7% of adolescents who develop major depressive disorder may commit suicide as young adults.	True False
8. Bipolar Disorder is characterized by mood swings.	True False
9. Youth and adults experience the same depressive symptoms.	True False
10. Bipolar Disorder is the same as Major Depressive Disorder.	True False

Table 14.1b Answers to Childhood Depression Quiz

1. False. While many clinicians maintain that infants, children, and adolescents can't get depressed due to ego capacities that are not fully developed, research indicates that up to 2.5% of children and 8.3% of adolescents in the U.S. suffer from depression (Birmaher et al., 1996).
2. False. Treatment for depression among children and adolescents has been shown to be highly effective.
3. True. Early intervention is a very effective course of action and can help mitigate the development of future problems.
4. False. It is estimated that 66% of children and adolescents with mental health problems do not get treatment (U.S. Department of Health and Human Services; 1998).
5. False. It is estimated that at least 25% of youth could benefit from mental health intervention when stress and risk factors are considered (Dryfoos, 1994).
6. True. Suicide is a risk factor among 10-to-24 year-olds (Hoyert, et al., 1997).
7. True. Suicide is a risk factor associated with major depressive disorder (Weissman et al., 1999).
8. True. Bipolar disorder is characterized by mood swings that include the highs of a manic episode and the lows of the depressive phase.
9. False. Symptoms of depression can look quite different among youth in comparison to adults.
10. False. While both are types of depression, bipolar disorder is characterized by shifts in mood, energy, and functioning while major depressive disorder is characterized by low mood.

DISCUSSION POINTS

After completing the quiz, discuss the following questions with your class:

1. What surprised you about the quiz?
2. What is your response to the reality that many depressed youth do not receive treatment?
3. How will you initiate a dialogue with the parents of a student you believe suffers from depression?
4. What is your role as an educator in terms of these issues?

DIVERSITY TRAINING ACTIVITY 14.2

STUDENT SCENARIO: RECOGNIZING THE WARNING SIGNS OF ANOREXIA NERVOSA

RATIONALE

A student in your class may have an eating disorder and not receive any type of intervention. The student may become increasingly symptomatic to the point that academic work suffers and social relationships become problematic. *Diversity Training Activity 14.2* illustrates the gradual decline of a student's classroom performance as her symptoms intensify. The following scenario helps you think through how to respond when faced with this type of classroom situation.

STEPS TO IMPLEMENTATION

1. Your instructor will divide the class into small groups of 5 to 6 students.
2. Read and review the scenario presented below:

> *Sophia is a 17-year-old high school student who has always been an active participant in the life of her school. A talented musician, Sophia has been a member of the marching band since her freshman year and plays in the school orchestra for drama club productions. Sophia receives good grades and has a 3.6 grade point average (GPA). Like her classmates, she is in the midst of applying to college. Her first choice college is a prestigious school located miles from home. She is drawn to the college because of its academic rigor and focus on music. She also thinks that being far away from home will help her transition away from her family.*
>
> *Sophia's parents prefer that she attend the local college in their area. They have the finances to pay for the more expensive school, but want Sophia close, should any crisis occur at home. Two years ago, Sophia's father was unexpectedly diagnosed with cancer. While he is in remission, the family lives in fear that the cancer will return. Sophia feels caught between the pressures to excel versus being there for her family. She feels confused because her parents always commended her on doing well. Now that Sophia has a chance to prove herself beyond home and her surrounding community, she feels she is being held back. These complicated feelings make Sophia feel guilty. She thinks if she was truly*

a good daughter, she would attend the local college to stay close to her family.

During the first semester of her senior year in high school, Sophia becomes acutely aware of her weight. Because she is grappling with the thought of going out into the world, she suddenly becomes quite critical of her appearance. Her mother was always overweight and seemed unhappy about choosing to be a housewife rather than pursue a career. Thinking she does not want to meet a similar destiny, Sophia decides to go on a diet. Initially innocent in her endeavor, Sophia becomes increasingly invested in the types of foods she eats, her caloric intake, and weight loss. She begins to eat less and weigh herself more. Sophia knows her parents will disapprove so she wears baggy clothing to hide her weight loss. At lunch she looks at the calories listed on the back of packaged foods and starts to drink water instead of juice or soda.

The issue of weight becomes an intense focus for Sophia. It seems the more weight she loses, the more she fears that it will return. Then something else begins to occur. Even though Sophia recognizes she has lost substantial weight, she starts to feel fat and overweight. Not eating enough to obtain a baseline of energy, Sophia appears tired and listless in the classroom. She has difficulty paying attention to the teacher and completing classroom assignments.

Always the excellent student, you the teacher begin to notice changes in Sophia's demeanor and appearance. She is definitely thinner and seems more secretive. Previously open and conversant, Sophia appears more closed off, as though carrying a burden. Sophia's grades have dropped, but you believe this is due to the pressures of the college application process.

School closes for winter break and you feel Sophia will be fine after a much needed vacation. Upon her return to class two weeks later, you are aghast at how thin Sophia looks. Being apart for two weeks has helped you see the culmination of her weight loss. Sophia's performance continues to drop and she shocks you when she gets an F grade on an in-class quiz. You approach her to talk about the grade but Sophia is reticent. In fact, she has become so isolated that she only spends time with a few classmates and has said she is thinking about not being in the orchestra for the spring play.

3. Talk about the following discussion points in your small groups and then with the entire class.

DISCUSSION POINTS

As Sophia's teacher you grapple with how to handle the above scenario. Consider the following as you come to terms with what to do about Sophia:

1. What warning signs suggest that Sophia is suffering from something other than stress associated with the college application process?
2. What role should you the teacher take in this situation?
3. Who will you talk to first--Sophia, the principal, or Sophia's parents?
4. How will you initiate a conversation with Sophia, the principal, and Sophia's parents?
5. How can you contribute to Sophia's well-being?

NOTEBOOK SECTION FOR CHAPTER 14

EXCEPTIONAL MICROCULTURES:
YOUTH WITH EMOTIONAL DISTURBANCE-
CHILDHOOD DEPRESSION, EATING DISORDERS

I. CONCEPTS/THEORIES

_____

_____

_____

_____

_____

_____

_____

_____

_____

_____

_____

_____

_____

_____

_____

_____

_____

_____

_____

_____

_____

_____

_____

II. CLASSROOM OBJECTIVES

III. BEST PRACTICES (HOW TO IMPLEMENT THOSE OBJECTIVES IN THE CLASSROOM)

_____

_____

_____

_____

_____

_____

_____

_____

_____

_____

_____

_____

_____

_____

_____

_____

_____

_____

_____

_____

_____

_____

_____

_____

_____

_____

WEB RESOURCES

- The American Academy of Child and Adolescent Psychiatry (AACAP) has a section of their Website called "Facts for Families." You can click on topic headings for fact sheets that provide information about a range of problems that have an impact on families such as adoption, grief, separation anxiety, grandparents raising grandchildren, and many more. Fact sheets are available in English, Spanish, French, Dutch, Polish, and Icelandic. The link to the Website is: http://www.aacap.org/publications/factsfam/index.htm
- The United States Department of Health and Human Services Substance Abuse and Mental Health Services Administration (SAMHSA) has an online national mental health information center. The Website provides up-to-date information about various mental health topics such as anxiety, children's mental health, youth violence prevention, and suicide prevention. Mental health links and information in Spanish are provided. Relevant themes and their descriptions are also listed. The reader can click on the topic and a page of relevant information will appear. The link to the Website is: http://www.mentalhealth.org/

REFERENCES

American Psychiatric Association (1994). *Diagnostic and statistical manual of mental disorders* (4th ed.). Washington, DC: Author.

Birmaher, B., Brent, D.A., & Benson, R.S. (1998). Summary of the practice parameters for the assessment and treatment of children and adolescents with depressive disorders. *Journal of the American Academy of Child and Adolescent Psychiatry, 37*(11), 1234-1238.

Birmaher, B., Ryan, N.D., Williamson, D.E., Brent, D.A., Kaufman, J., Dahl, R.E., Perel, J., & Nelson, B. (1996). Childhood and adolescent depression: A review of the past ten years. Part I. *Journal of the American Academy of Child and Adolescent Psychiatry, 35*(11), 1427-1439.

Chua-Eoan, H. (1999, May 31). Escaping from the darkness. *Time*, 44-49.

Clauss-Ehlers, C.S., & Weist, M. (2002). Children are news worthy: Working effectively with the media to improve systems of child and adolescent mental health. In H. Ghuman, M.D. Weist, & R. Sarles (Eds.), *Providing mental health services to youth where they are: School and community-based approaches* (pp. 225-239). New York, NY: Brunner-Routledge.

Dryfoos, J. G. (1994). *Full-service schools: A revolution in health and social services for children, youth, and families*. San Francisco, CA: Jossey-Bass.

Freud, S. (1894). The neuro-psychoses of defense, Vol. 3, in *The standard edition of the complete psychological works of Sigmund Freud, Volumes I-XXIII* (1962, pp. 43-61), London: Hogarth Press.

Freud, S. (1896). Further remarks on the neuro-psychoses of defense, Vol. 3, in *The standard edition of the complete psychological works of Sigmund Freud, Volumes I-XXIII* (1962, pp. 159-185), London: Hogarth Press.

Gibbs, N. (1999, May 31). Time: Special report. *Time*, 33.

Hoyert, D.L., Kochanek, K.D., & Murphy, S.L. (1999). *Deaths: Final data for 1997. National Vital Statistics Report.* (Publication No. PHS 99-1120, 47(19)). Hyattsville: National Center for Health Statistics.

Klerman, G.L., & Weissman, M.M. (1989). Increasing rates of depression. *Journal of the American Medical Association, 261*(15), 2229-2235.

Kog, E., & Vandereycken, W. (1989). Family interaction in easting disorder patients and normal controls. *International Journal of Eating Disorders, 8*(1), 11-23.

United States Department of Health and Human Services (1998). *Systems of care: A promising solution for children with serious emotional disturbances and their families.* Washington, DC: Author.

Weissman, M.M., Wolk, S., Goldstein, R.B., Moreau, D., Adams, P., Greenwald, S., Klier, C.M., Ryan, N.D., Dahl, R.E., & Wickramaratne, P. (1999). Depressed adolescents grown up. *Journal of the American Medical Association, 281*(18), 1707-1713.

Chapter 15
Exceptional Microcultures: How to Make a Referral

Educators are uniquely qualified to support the educational and emotional needs of our youth. Teachers are among the adults who spend the most time with our children. While your role is not to diagnose a child, you can certainly intervene and make a referral when necessary. Because you spend substantial classroom time with your students, you will often be the first to notice changes in a student's mood or behavior.

The purpose of this chapter is to help you feel you can intervene when potential problems are identified. Positive mental health is not something that begins for a child after the school day is over. An appropriate referral means problems are addressed quickly and appropriately. Making a timely referral is one way to intervene before problems get worse.

Chapter 15 focuses on how to make an effective referral. Teachers who feel more comfortable and confident with the referral process will be more likely to refer students. While this statement seems straightforward enough, I was surprised to learn how little literature actually discusses how to refer students for mental health services. The British Columbia Ministry of Education has a Website that addresses how teachers can refer students with Attention Deficit Hyperactivity Disorder (ADHD) (Government of British Columbia, Ministry of Education, Special Education, n.d.). The British Columbia model presents a step-by-step process where the teacher acquires information and considers strategies soon after noticing the student is having difficulty in class. In this model, a referral is made only when other learning strategies have been implemented and are unsuccessful.

While making a referral after educational strategies have been used is appropriate for students with special education needs, students with mental health problems require more expedient intervention. There are many situations that suggest a referral may be needed. A student may continue to struggle in class or someone may not interact with peers as he did before. Perhaps your straight A student appears depressed over a period of time and starts to engage in self-destructive behaviors. Table 15.1 provides a model that you can follow when you need to refer a student for mental health services.

Table 15.1 Who to Consult When a Student Needs Assistance

Level of Referral	An Educator's Step-By-Step Guide to the Referral Process
Consult with the school principal	A first step in the referral process is to talk with the principal about the problems you have observed in class. Key questions to consider are: Is there a referral process already in place in the school where I teach? What kind of documentation about the problem should I show the parent? How long has the problem existed? Who should be present when concerns about the child are discussed with the parent?
Talk with the parent(s) or guardian	It is important to inform parents about what is going on with their child. Children under 18 years of age cannot be seen for psychotherapy without parental consent. Talk with the parent(s) or guardian about your concerns. Discuss the symptoms you have observed in the classroom. Provide parents with literature that further explains your observations. Work with parents and the school to get the referral process underway.
Informal Collaboration	You the teacher, with parental support and awareness, can collaborate with school personnel such as the school mental health professional, the guidance counselor, referral sources, and the principal. Parental consent is needed for school personnel to speak with outside sources.
Referral to School-Based Mental Health Professional, District or Community-Based Services	The school-based mental health professional is the trained mental health professional in the school. District or community-based services include school psychologists who work in the school district or are contracted to provide assessment and ongoing services. Parental consent and permission is needed.
Parent Referral to Community-Based Services	A referral is made to a psychologist, mental health professional, or community-based clinic. Community-based services include mental health clinics, private practitioners, or mental health services provided by the local hospital. The service provider can conduct a thorough evaluation to determine the course of treatment for the child or adolescent.

Good communication skills are an essential part of the referral process. Talking with parents about their child's problem is a sensitive conversation. Showing concern and empathy helps foster an ongoing dialogue with the child's parent(s) or guardian. Remember that it is better to talk to parents about what you see instead of ignoring the problem. Many of my students say that they don't know how to start a conversation with parents about their child's problem. They are being honest when they share that they want to ignore the problem, hope it goes away, or wait until the problem escalates and can no longer be ignored. These alternatives don't work. They are unresponsive and set the child up for failure.

The following *Diversity Training Activities* underscore how you can take a more proactive stance with regard to your students' well-being. Being proactive is particularly important in light of research that shows early intervention promotes better mental health outcomes (Clauss-Ehlers & Weist, 2004; Kumpfer, 1999). The activities below address the discomfort both new and veteran teachers experience when faced with having to talk to a parent about troubling behaviors. *Diversity Training Activity 15.1, Effective Referral Communication,* focuses on elements of good communication when the referral is made. *Diversity Training Activity 15.2, Student Scenario: Referring Paul for Treatment,* presents a situation where a student needs to be referred for treatment. Participants role-play how they will talk with the principal, the child, the parent, and the referral source. As you engage in both *Diversity Training Activities* recognize that the ability to make an appropriate referral is a skill that comes with experience and practice.

DIVERSITY TRAINING ACTIVITY 15.1
EFFECTIVE REFERRAL COMMUNICATION

RATIONALE

Diversity Training Activity 15.1 is designed to increase your awareness about how to be an effective communicator when you have to make a referral. Being able to talk with parents about why a referral is needed is particularly important given the sensitive nature of this conversation. *Diversity Training Activity 15.1* introduces you to the skills associated with making a referral so that you can include this ability as part of your teaching repertoire.

STEPS TO IMPLEMENTATION

1. Your instructor will lead the class discussion about how to be an effective communicator when you have to make a referral.
2. Review Table 15.2 *Making a Referral: Elements of Effective Communication* before you begin your discussion.

Table 15.2 Making a Referral: Elements of Effective Communication

Effective Communication with the Child/Adolescent	Effective Communication with the Parent/Guardian
Begin the referral conversation with a focus on the positive. The conversation with the child/adolescent is likely to occur with the parent present so expect to go back and forth between the two skill sets presented in this table.	Begin the conversation with a focus on what you like about being the child's/adolescent's teacher and what she brings to the classroom.
From a focus on the positive, begin a discussion about the troubling behavior you have observed.	From your discussion about positive qualities, talk honestly but supportively about the troubling behavior you have observed.
Talk about the behaviors the child engages in, rather than equate the child/adolescent with these behaviors (i.e., Say: "Your behavior disrupts the class," rather than "You as a person disrupt the class").	Do not equate the child/adolescent with the behavior when talking to the parent/guardian. Discuss the behavior as something the child/adolescent does (i.e., Say: "Your child's behavior has disrupted the class," rather than "Your child/adolescent disrupts the class").
At this point in the conversation, give the child/adolescent the opportunity to respond and share her perspective. You may begin this part of the conversation with an open-ended question such as, "What are your thoughts about this?"	At this point in the conversation, allow the parent or guardian to share his perspective. You might elicit this with a question such as, "What is your reaction to the information I am sharing with you?" or "Have you noticed similar changes in your child's behavior at home?"
Listen to the child/adolescent in an empathic manner. The child/adolescent may have a completely different viewpoint about the problem. It is critical to hear, acknowledge, and incorporate that perspective as you work towards an appropriate referral.	Actively listen to the parent or guardian's response. Is there agreement with your observation? Is there denial? What appears to be the level of commitment to work with you to get the child/adolescent help? Showing empathy will help the parent or guardian feel heard, less judged, and recognize your goal is to work together as a team.
After truly hearing the child's/adolescent's response, talk about the ways in which getting help can be a starting point for feeling better. Share that you understand it may be scary to think about talking to a stranger, but that you will offer your support throughout the process.	Establish a working alliance as you listen to the parent or guardian's concerns. Because referral and treatment depends upon parental cooperation, a mutual partnership is critical at this time. For those parents who struggle to acknowledge their child's difficulty, suggest they talk with the school counselor for additional information about the problem.
Talk with the child/adolescent about the referral process. This does not need to be a long discussion, but can simply inform the child/adolescent about what to expect. This conversation will most likely occur in tandem with the child's parent or guardian. Let everyone know you are available for ongoing conversation about the referral.	Talk with the parent or guardian about what to expect from the referral process. Advise them of referral and treatment options. If you are not privy to this information, prepare them for a conversation with the school mental health professional or guidance counselor. Reassure the parent that you can be contacted as needed.

DISCUSSION POINTS

Consider the following questions that relate to effective components of the referral process:

1. What makes you most nervous talking to parents or guardians, youth, and school personnel about a child or adolescent who needs a referral?
2. What strengths will you bring to conversations about the referral process?
3. What will be most difficult when you talk with parents or guardians about a problem you observe in their child or adolescent?
4. Who will you consult if you feel uncomfortable having this conversation?
5. Who should be present when you have this conversation?

DIVERSITY TRAINING ACTIVITY 15.2

STUDENT SCENARIO: REFERRING PAUL FOR TREATMENT

RATIONALE

The purpose of *Diversity Training Activity 15.2* is to help you practice your communication skills in a referral situation. In the scenario presented below, Paul's situation becomes increasingly apparent as his teacher reads his response to an essay question on an exam. In this activity you will practice talking to the principal, the parent, the student, and the referral source about Paul's problems.

STEPS TO IMPLEMENTATION: PART I

1. Read Paul's response to a question on an essay exam below.
2. Paul's Essay

> *The origins of witchcraft began in 1692 with experiments of fortune telling. In Essex County, especially Salem Village in Massachusetts, girls got together and talked about the future. One of the girls made a crystal ball and saw the image of a coffin. The parents of the girls started to notice their strange behavior. A minister asked a physician to look at the girls. I don't know if what I'm writing makes sense. This is off the topic*

but I wanted to share something about what's going on with me. I'm not going to do well on this test. I feel I am always failing. Maybe killing myself is one way to cope. I can do it before my mom comes in to talk with the teacher this Friday for the parent/teacher conference. The teacher will say that I have problems. She'll ask my mom to talk to me but my mom won't do anything. She'll say that this is my education and that I'm responsible—like she always does. I don't know if I'm ever going to do things the right way.

DISCUSSION POINTS: PART I

Your instructor will go around the room and ask how you feel about Paul's essay. Perhaps you are shocked by Paul's answer and have no idea how to respond. Perhaps you have a sense of what to do in this situation but are not sure it's the best course of action. These are normal reactions to an adolescent in crisis. Questions participants have raised with me after reading such scenarios are:

1. What is my responsibility as a teacher?
2. What if the parent says this child doesn't have a problem?
3. What am I responsible for legally?
4. What if I don't do anything?
5. What if I don't feel qualified to talk to the parent alone, can I bring an administrator in to talk with me?
6. How can I tell the difference between fantasy and the child's reality?
7. Should I take this student seriously?
8. Do I have to tell the parent what is going on with this student?

STEPS TO IMPLEMENTATION: PART II

The second part of *Diversity Training Activity 15.2* is to role-play Paul's teacher. Consider how you will talk about the essay to Paul, his parents or guardians, the principal, and the person or place you refer Paul to for treatment.

1. Pair up with the person sitting next to you in class.
2. Take turns being the teacher and playing each of the following roles:
- Dyad I. Role-play what you the teacher will say to Paul.
  (Roles= Teacher and Paul).
- Dyad II. Role-play what you the teacher will say to the parent or guardian.

(Roles=Teacher and parent or guardian).
- Dyad III. Role-play what you the teacher will say to the principal. (Roles=Teacher and principal).
- Dyad IV. Role-play what you the teacher will say to the referral source. (Roles=Teacher and referral source).
3. After each exchange, your instructor will select one dyad to conduct their role-play in front of the class.

DISCUSSION POINTS: PART II

After each dyad is modeled for the class, discuss the following:

1. What did you like about how the role-play was handled?
2. What would you have done differently?
3. What was it like to deal with Paul's situation as a teacher?
4. What was easiest for you to do in this scenario?
5. What was most difficult?
6. How will you deal with similar situations in the future?

NOTEBOOK SECTION FOR CHAPTER 15

EXCEPTIONAL MICROCULTURES:
HOW TO MAKE A REFERRAL

I. CONCEPTS/THEORIES

_____

_____

_____

_____

_____

_____

_____

_____

_____

_____

_____

_____

_____

_____

_____

_____

_____

_____

_____

_____

II. CLASSROOM OBJECTIVES

_____

_____

_____

_____

_____

_____

_____

_____

_____

_____

_____

_____

_____

_____

_____

_____

_____

_____

_____

_____

_____

_____

_____

III. BEST PRACTICES (HOW TO IMPLEMENT THOSE OBJECTIVES IN THE CLASSROOM)

_____

_____

_____

_____

_____

_____

_____

_____

_____

_____

_____

_____

_____

_____

_____

_____

_____

_____

_____

_____

_____

_____

_____

_____

_____

_____

_____

WEB RESOURCES

- Scholastic provides an overview of when teachers need to consult an expert, how to assess the need for help, and steps involved in the referral process. The link to the Website is: http://teacher.scholastic.com/professional/todayschild/consultexpert.htm
- The Southern Derbyshire Health Services Web Portal provides an example of questions parents frequently ask when their child is being given a referral. The Website focuses on referrals for speech and language development. The questions often asked by parents, however, apply to many referral situations and include: What will happen once a referral is made? What happens when my child is seen for assessment? What happens if my child needs services? How long will my child need services? The link for the Website is: http://www.southernderbyshire.nhs.uk/speech/faq_children.asp

REFERENCES

Clauss-Ehlers, C.S., & Weist, M.D. (Eds.). (2004). *Community planning to foster resilience in children*. New York, NY: Kluwer Academic Publishers.

Government of British Columbia, Ministry of Education, Special Education (n.d.). *Teaching students with Attention-Deficit/Hyperactivity Disorder.* Retrieved November 14, 2004, from http://www.bced.gov.bc.ca/specialed/adhd/address.htm

Kumpfer, K.L. (1999). Factors and processes contributing to resilience: The resilience framework. In M.D. Glantz & J.L. Johnson (Eds.), *Resilience and development: Positive life adaptations* (pp. 179-224). New York, NY: Kluwer Academic Publishers.

Section 6

Conclusion

Chapter 16

Conclusion:
The Multicultural Educator

At the beginning of this book I talked about teaching as a relationship. Sixteen chapters later we have come full circle in thinking about that relationship as one that reaches out, grabs, and embraces diversity. We have learned how teaching for diversity lays the foundation for multicultural education. We have examined, analyzed, and explored dimensions of diversity within ourselves, others, and in the systems around us. We have considered challenges to diversity such as how to deal with racism, curriculums that espouse only one perspective, and unsafe classroom environments that result from poor management, bullying, and homophobia. We have explored exceptional microcultures and looked at your response to trauma, abuse, and mental health problems. The ability to make an appropriate referral has been discussed as a critical skill for helping students. We have integrated theory and practice through a review of research, discussion about current educational realities, and participation in *Diversity Training Activities*. It is hoped that these efforts have made you feel more confident about your ability to deal with the many multicultural issues in today's pluralistic school system.

An important caveat, however, is that this text presents only one model of multicultural education. The current model discusses many important aspects of diversity, but is not exhaustive of all dimensions of difference. While it is beyond the scope of this book to cover all areas, you are encouraged to seek out theory, research, and practical applications on topics like able-bodiness, age, other mental health problems, religion, learning styles, learning disabilities, and many more.

Whatever the topic at hand, the current text has focused on helping you develop an open and flexible worldview to bring to any dimension of diversity. From a perspective of cognitive and emotional flexibility, it is hoped that you will not impose values that conflict with those of other groups, but strive to intervene in a culturally relevant manner. This ability takes ongoing awareness, understanding, and the desire to always learn more about what it means to truly embrace differences.

Understanding and accepting individuals and families from diverse backgrounds means that you are willing to be changed and affected by them. The practice of multicultural education does not mean you have to "get it right" all the time. Rather, an effective multicultural educator is someone who can graciously acknowledge when he or she has made a mistake and work to recover from it. If you are uncertain about how to deal with a particular situation, being open to supervision is a skill in and of itself.

All of this is to say that the practice of multicultural education does not happen alone. Seeking out information, appropriate resources, and furthering your own understanding are critical components of effective multicultural education practice. *Diversity Training Activity 16.1, Your Personal Statement About Being a Multicultural Educator,* is designed to help you think through your identity as a multicultural educator. *Diversity Training Activity 16.2, Self-Inventory for Educators Promoting Multicultural Efforts in Schools,* is geared to help you assess your strengths and weaknesses in future multicultural efforts. In sum, multicultural education is defined as follows:

"a philosophical concept built on the ideals of freedom, justice, equality, equity, and human dignity...It values cultural differences and affirms the pluralism that students, their communities, and teachers reflect. It challenges all forms of discrimination in schools and society through the promotion of democratic principles of social justice. Multicultural education is a process that permeates all aspects of school practices, policies and organization as a means to ensure the highest levels of academic achievement for all students. It helps students develop a positive self-concept by providing knowledge about the histories, cultures, and contributions of diverse groups. It prepares all students to work actively toward structural equality in organizations and institutions by providing the knowledge, dispositions, and skills for the redistribution of power and income among diverse groups. Thus, school curriculum must directly address issues of racism, sexism, classism, linguicism, ablism, ageism, heterosexism, religious intolerance, and xenophobia. Multicultural education advocates the belief that students and their life histories and experiences should be placed at the center of the teaching and learning process and that pedagogy should occur in a context that is familiar to students and that addresses multiple ways of thinking. In addition, teachers and students must critically analyze oppression and power relations in their communities, society and the world. To accomplish these goals, multicultural education demands a school staff that is culturally competent, and to the greatest extent possible racially, culturally, and linguistically diverse. Staff must be multiculturally literate and capable of including and embracing families and communities to create an environment that is supportive of multiple perspectives, experiences, and democracy" (National Association for Multicultural Education [NAME], 2003).

As you end this part of your training, important points to keep in mind as you further your development as a multicultural educator are:

- Self-awareness is an important aspect of effective multicultural education practice.
- A flexible worldview can be transferred to many diverse situations.
- "Getting it right" is sometimes not as important as making up for how you "got it wrong."
- If you are uncertain about how to deal with a particular situation, seek out consultation or supervision. This is an act of ethics and professionalism, not incompetence.
- Effective multicultural education does not happen in a vacuum but in a context of community-building, advocacy, and resource-gathering.
- The work you've done via this book is just a starting point.
- Being an effective multicultural educator is a lifelong process.

DIVERSITY TRAINING ACTIVITY 16.1

YOUR PERSONAL STATEMENT ABOUT BEING A MULTICULTURAL EDUCATOR

RATIONALE

This book has prompted you to think about the meaning of multicultural education, your role in multicultural efforts, and how you envision yourself as an active participant in school life. You have been challenged to think about the complexity and skill associated with the many issues that lie at the heart of diversity. At the core of this challenge lies the question: "How do you perceive yourself as a multicultural educator?" With so many diverse issues at play in today's school setting, how do you view your own particular style and contribution to multicultural efforts? The following *Diversity Training Activity* is geared to help you think about your identity as a multicultural educator.

STEPS TO IMPLEMENTATION

1. *Diversity Training Activity 16.1* can be conducted as an in-class or out-of-class assignment.

2. Write an essay that discusses your self-concept as a multicultural educator. Talk about your own dimensions of difference and how they influence your work as an educator. Consider your strengths and weaknesses and their implications for work in a multicultural educational setting.

DISCUSSION POINTS

Whether you completed the assignment in class or on your own, take a moment to discuss the following points about multicultural education with your peers:

1. What did you learn about yourself by writing this essay?
2. How do you describe your particular style as a multicultural educator?
3. What particular dimensions of diversity do you feel most comfortable with and why?
4. What dimensions of diversity do you feel the least comfortable with and why?

Remember that being a multicultural educator does not mean you must have expertise in every dimension of diversity. Rather, it means that you are open and flexible when faced with different aspects of diversity. You are encouraged to seek consultation or supervision when faced with a dimension you know little or nothing about.

DIVERSITY TRAINING ACTIVITY 16.2

SELF-INVENTORY FOR EDUCATORS PROMOTING MULTICULTURAL EFFORTS IN SCHOOLS

RATIONALE

Diversity Training Activity 16.2 is a self-inventory designed to examine your thoughts, feelings, and commitment to the practice of multicultural education. The self-inventory covers each section reviewed in this book. The scoring procedure and analysis at the end of the self-inventory provide additional insight about your strengths and areas of growth as a multicultural educator.

STEPS TO IMPLEMENTATION

1. Table 16.1 presents the *Self-Inventory for Educators Promoting Multicultural Efforts in Schools.* If you are not currently in a school setting, base your responses on how you envision your future role as a multicultural educator. Add each item to get an overall score. Plot your score on the scale presented after Table 16.1.

Table 16.1 Self-Inventory for Educators Promoting Multicultural Efforts in Schools

Directions: Place a 1, 2, or 3 in front of each item. *Scoring:* 1=Would not promote this skill, knowledge, behavior, or attitude; 2=Would sometimes promote this skill, knowledge, behavior, or attitude; 3=Would often promote this skill, knowledge, behavior, or attitude.

Score	Understanding Difference
	1. I am careful not to impose my cultural values in ways that create conflict for people from other cultures.
	2. I include the diverse cultural values of students in my classroom.
	3. I try to be aware of how my biases influence learning.
	4. I encourage my students to engage in an ongoing dialogue about difference.
	5. I welcome greater awareness and understanding about student diversity.
	Dimensions of Difference
	6. I actively work to understand my worldview and its influence on lesson plans, classroom discussions, and student evaluations.
	7. Racist incidents are addressed immediately and followed with a dialogue about the behavior.
	8. I use bilingual professionals or professional interpreters when working with children who speak English as a second language.
	9. I reach out to families in ways that reflect their cultural frame of reference.
	10. I promote a school environment that is open to students with diverse sexual identities.
	Challenges to Diversity
	11. If a bullying incident occurs at school, I intervene and promote a non-violent policy.
	12. I work with bystanders to reduce bullying.
	13. I know the rules and regulations for mandated reporters in my school.
	14. I feel comfortable talking with my supervisor or principal about possible abuse or neglect experienced by my students.
	15. I am familiar with school factors that decrease disruptive behaviors and promote a positive learning environment.
	Understanding Exceptional Microcultures
	16. I am aware of the signs and symptoms of trauma and how they vary across different developmental stages.

Table 16.1 (continued) Self-Inventory for Educators Promoting Multicultural Efforts in Schools

	17. I understand how trauma can be culturally and contextually based.
	18. I can respond to a student who needs psychological intervention and treatment.
	19. I know about the referral sources in my school and in the surrounding community.
	20. I recognize the warning signs associated with child and adolescent depression.
	Multicultural Education Practices
	21. I understand that there are within-group differences as well as between-group differences, meaning that no group consists of members who are all exactly the same as one another.
	22. I am thoughtful about my approach to multicultural education.
	23. I engage in an ongoing dialogue with colleagues about best practices in the field of multicultural education.
	24. I strive to incorporate multicultural media and resources in the classroom.
	25. I seek out supervision when I don't have experience working with someone from a particular culture.

Scoring procedure and scale: *Take a moment and add up the total numerical result for the 25 items. Write your score here: _____ and plot it on the scale below:*

0	25	50	75

This scale helps you think about where you lie on the multicultural educator continuum. A higher scale score reflects greater openness and comfort grappling with the multicultural education issues presented in the text. The meanings of each score are as follows:

25. This is the lowest possible score you can get on the self-inventory. This score says you feel uncomfortable, lack confidence, or have a general lack of interest in promoting a multicultural school environment. You will benefit from additional training and skill-building focused on multicultural education. Talk with your instructor or supervisor about what you struggle with: Were there parts of the text that you found particularly challenging? What Diversity Training Activities were most difficult? How do you see yourself as a future multicultural educator?

26-50. These scores are in the middle range of the self-inventory. They suggest that you are ambivalent about multicultural education. Perhaps you feel insecure about your ability to deal with the many situations presented in the text: Is it difficult to think about yourself as a multicultural educator? Are there some areas you are stronger in than others? Keep in mind that multicultural education involves life long learning. Seek out additional training and educational experiences that will build on your strengths and further develop areas of growth.

51-75. These scores are at the top end of the self-inventory. Scores in this range say you identify with the multicultural educator's role. You are open to the dimensions of diversity discussed throughout the book and willing to take risks when called upon to implement your skills. It is important to keep in mind, however, that this text presents one framework for multicultural education practice. There are other dimensions of diversity not covered in the text that you are bound to work with in the classroom. You are encouraged to continue your development as a multicultural educator by seeking out mentors, supervisors, and educational opportunities that build on your interest, commitment, and vision.

DISCUSSION POINTS

1. What was your reaction to your overall score on the *Self-Inventory for Educators Promoting Multicultural Efforts in Schools*?
2. What dimensions of diversity do you feel more comfortable dealing with? How do you understand the greater sense of comfort you feel in these domains?
3. Are there areas where you feel less confident about your ability as a multicultural educator? How do you understand the discomfort associated with these areas?
4. What hopes do you have for yourself as a multicultural educator?
5. Multicultural education is an ongoing process of awareness, understanding, knowledge, and skill-building. What are your thoughts about seeking out additional training and education?

NOTEBOOK SECTION FOR CHAPTER 16
CONCLUSION: THE MULTICULTURAL EDUCATOR

I. CONCEPTS/THEORIES

_____

_____

_____

_____

_____

_____

_____

_____

_____

_____

_____

_____

_____

_____

_____

_____

_____

_____

_____

_____

_____

II. CLASSROOM OBJECTIVES

III. BEST PRACTICES (HOW TO IMPLEMENT THOSE OBJECTIVES IN THE CLASSROOM)

_____

_____

_____

_____

_____

_____

_____

_____

_____

_____

_____

_____

_____

_____

_____

_____

_____

_____

_____

_____

_____

_____

_____

WEB RESOURCES

- The National Association of School Psychologists (NASP) has devoted an entire section of their Website to culturally competent practice. These Web pages include definitions of culture, cultural competence, and a discussion about how to provide culturally competent services. Culturally-focused resources are also provided that deal with topics like crisis response, consultant work, and English language learners. The link to the cultural competence section of the NASP Website is: http://www.nasponline.org/culturalcompetence/index.html

REFERENCES

National Association for Multicultural Education (2003, February 1). *Resolutions and position papers: Multicultural education.* Retrieved April 11, 2005, from http://www.nameorg.org/resolutions/definition.html

Selected Bibliography

SECTION 1. FOUNDATIONS

CHAPTER 1. INTRODUCTION: HOW TO USE THIS MANUAL

Banks, J.A., & McGee Banks, C.A. (2004). *Multicultural education* (5th ed.). Hoboken, NJ: John Wiley & Sons, Inc.

Gollnick, D. M., & Chinn, P.C. (2001*). Multicultural education in a pluralistic society* (6th ed.). Upper Saddle River, NJ: Prentice Hall.

Manning, M.L., & Baruth, L.G. (2004*). Multicultural education of children and adolescents* (4th ed.). Boston, MA: Pearson Education, Inc.

Nieto, S. (2004). *Affirming diversity: The sociopolitical context of multicultural education* (4th ed.). New York, NY: Pearson Education, Inc.

Spring, J. (2001). *Deculturalization and the struggle for equality: A brief history of the education of dominated cultures in the United States* (3rd ed.). New York, NY: McGraw Hill.

CHAPTER 2. HOW DO WE UNDERSTAND DIFFERENCE?

Koppelman, K.L., & Goodhart, R.L. (2005). *Understanding human differences: Multicultural education for diverse America.* New York, NY: Pearson Education, Inc.

Phinney, J.S. (1996). When we talk about American ethnic groups, what do we mean*? American Psychologist, 51* (9), 918-927.

SECTION 2. DIMENSIONS OF DIFFERENCE: CULTURE, SOCIOECONOMIC STATUS, RACE, ETHNICITY, LANGUAGE, AND PARENTAL PARTNERSHIP

CHAPTER 3. CULTURAL VALUES AND WORLDVIEW

Diller, J.V., & Moule, J. (2005). *Cultural competence: A primer for educators.* Belmont, CA: Thomson Wadsworth.

Frow, J. (1995). *Cultural studies and cultural values.* New York, NY: Oxford University Press.

Kluckhohn, F.R, & Strodtbeck, F.L. (1961). *Variations in value orientations.* Evanston, IL: Row, Peterson, & Co.

CHAPTER 4. SOCIOECONOMIC STATUS

Cohen, E.G., & Lotan, R.A. (Eds.). (1997). *Working for equity in heterogeneous classrooms: Sociological theory in practice.* New York, NY: Teachers College Press.
Lareau, A. (2000). *Home advantage: Social class and parental intervention in elementary education.* New York, NY: Rowman & Littlefield Publishers, Inc.
Oakes, J. (1985). *Keeping track: How schools structure inequality.* New Haven, CT: Yale University Press.

CHAPTER 5. RACE AND ETHNICITY

Ausdale, D.V., & Feagin, J.R. (2001). *The first R: How children learn race and racism.* New York, NY: Rowman & Littlefield Publishers, Inc.
Helms. J. (1994). Racial identity in the school environment. In P. Pedersen & J.C. Carey (Eds.), *Multicultural counseling in schools: A practical handbook* (pp. 19-38). Boston, MA: Allyn & Bacon.
Javier, R.A., & Camacho-Gingerich, A. (2004). Risk and resilience in Latino youth. In C.S. Clauss-Ehlers & M.D. Weist (Eds.), *Community planning to foster resilience in children* (pp. 65-81). New York, NY: Kluwer Academic Publishers.
LaFromboise, T., & Medoff, L. (2004). Sacred spaces: The role of context in American Indian youth development. In C.S. Clauss-Ehlers & M.D. Weist (Eds.), *Community planning to foster resilience in children* (pp.45-63). New York, NY: Kluwer Academic Publishers.
LaGrange, R.D. (2004). Building strengths in inner city African-American children: The task and promise of schools. In C.S. Clauss-Ehlers & M.D. Weist (Eds.), *Community planning to foster resilience in children (*pp. 83-97). New York, NY: Kluwer Academic Publishers.
Shimahora, N.K., Holowinsky, I.Z., & Tomlinson-Clarke, S. (2001). *Ethnicity, race, and nationality in education.* Mahwah, NJ: Lawrence Erlbaum Associates.
Wong, G. (2004). Resilience in the Asian context. In C.S. Clauss-Ehlers & M.D. Weist (Eds.), *Community planning to foster resilience in children (*pp. 99-111). New York, NY: Kluwer Academic Publishers.

CHAPTER 6. LANGUAGE IN THE CLASSROOM

Clauss, C.S. (1998). Language: The unspoken variable in psychotherapy practice. *Psychotherapy, 35* (2), 188-196.
LaFromboise, T., Colman, H.L.K., & Gerton, T. (1993). Psychological impact of biculturalism: Evidence and theory. *Psychological Bulletin, 114* (3), 395-412.
Ovando, C.J., & McLaren, P. (Eds.). (2000). *The politics of multiculturalism and bilingual education: Students and teachers caught in the cross fire.* Boston, MA: McGraw-Hill.

CHAPTER 7. WORKING WITH DIVERSE FAMILIES: PARENTAL PARTNERSHIP IN EDUCATION

Eccles, J.S., Midgley, C., Wigfield, A., Buchanan, M., Reuman, D., Flanagan, C., & MacIver, D. (1993). Development during adolescence: The impact of stage-environment fit on young adolescents' experiences in schools and in families. *American Psychologist, 48*(2), 90-101.

Melendez, M.C., & Tomlinson-Clarke, S. (2004). Home, school, and community: Catalysts to resilience. In C.S. Clauss-Ehlers & M.D. Weist (Eds.), *Community planning to foster resilience in children* (pp. 311-325). New York, NY: Kluwer Academic Publishers.

Tseng, W.S., & Hsu, J.L. (1991). Culture and family assessment. In W.S. Tseng & J.L. Hsu (Eds.), *Culture and family: Problems and therapy* (pp. 171-191). New York, NY: Haworth Press.

SECTION 3. DIMENSIONS OF DIFFERENCE: GENDER

CHAPTER 8. GENDER

American Association of University Women Educational Foundation (AAUW). (1993). *Hostile hallways: The AAUW survey of sexual harassment in America's schools.* Washington, D.C.: Author.

Bailey, S.M. (2002). *The Jossey-Bass reader on gender in education.* Hoboken, NJ: Jossey-Bass.

Diller, A., Houston, B., Morgan, K.P., & Avim, M. (1996). *The gender question in education: Theory, pedagogy, and politics.* Boulder, CO: Westview Press.

U.S. Department of Education. (2000). *U.S. Department of Education's gender equity expert panel exemplary and promising gender equity programs* (SuDoc ED 1.310/2:457116). Washington, D.C.: U.S. Dept. of Education, Office of Educational Research and Improvement, Educational Resources Information Center.

CHAPTER 9. SEXUAL ORIENTATION AND YOUTH

Anderson, D.A. (1994). Lesbian and gay adolescents: Social and developmental considerations. *The High School Journal, 77*, 13-19.

Powers, B., & Ellis, A. (1996). *A family and friend's guide to sexual orientation: Bridging the divide between gay and straight.* Oxford, UK: Routledge.

Reynolds, A.L., & Koski, M.J. (1994). Lesbian, gay and bisexual teens and the school counselor: Building alliances. *The High School Journal, 77*, 88-94.

SECTION 4. OTHER CHALLENGES TO DIVERSITY

CHAPTER 10. BULLYING IN SCHOOLS

Beane, A.L. (1999). *The bully free classroom: Over 100 tips and strategies for teachers K-8.* Minneapolis, MN: Free Spirit Publishing.

Coloroso, B. (2004). *The bully, the bullied, and the bystander: From preschool to high school--how parents and teachers can help break the cycle of violence.* New York, NY: HarperResource.

Olweus, D. (1993). *Bullying at school: What we know and what we can do.* Malden, MA: Blackwell Publishers.

CHAPTER 11. CREATING COMMUNITY THROUGH CLASSROOM MANAGEMENT

Poland, S. (1997). School crisis teams. In A.P. Goldstein & J.C. Conoly (Eds.*), School violence interventions: A practical handbook* (pp. 127-159). New York, NY: The Guilford Press.

Seeman, H. (1999). *Preventing classroom management problems: A classroom management handbook* (3rd ed.). Lanham, MD: Scarecrow Press.

Stephan, S.H., Mathur, S., & Owens, C.S. (2004). School strategies to prevent and address youth gang involvement. In C.S. Clauss-Ehlers & M.D. Weist (Eds.), *Community planning to foster resilience in children* (pp. 217-232). New York, NY: Kluwer Academic Publishers.

Studer, J. (1996). Understanding and preventing aggressive responses in youth. *Elementary School Guidance and Counseling, 30*, 194-203.

CHAPTER 12. CHILD ABUSE AND RESILIENCE

Clauss-Ehlers, C.S. (2004). Re-inventing resilience: A model of "culturally-focused resilient adaptation." In C.S. Clauss-Ehlers & M.D. Weist (Eds.), *Community planning to foster resilience in children (*pp. 27-41). New York, NY: Kluwer Academic Publishers.

Lynch, M., & Cicchetti, D. (1997). Children's relationships with adults and peers: An examination of elementary and junior high school students. *Journal of School Psychology, 35*(1), 81-99.

Newberger, C.M., & Gremy, I.M. (2004). Clinical and institutional interventions and children's resilience and recovery from sexual abuse. In C.S. Clauss-Ehlers & M.D. Weist, (Eds.), *Community planning to foster resilience in children (*pp. 197-215). New York, NY: Kluwer Academic Publishers.

Pianta, R.C., & Walsh, D.J. (1998). Applying the construct of resilience in schools: Cautions from a developmental systems perspective. *School Psychology Review, 27* (3), 407-417.

SECTION 5. UNDERSTANDING EXCEPTIONAL MICROCULTURES

CHAPTER 13. EXCEPTIONAL MICROCULTURES: DEALING WITH TRAUMA

Ciechalski, J.C., & Schmidt, M.W. (1995). The effects of social skills training on students with exceptionalities. *Elementary School Guidance and Counseling, 29*, 217-222.

Clauss-Ehlers, C.S., Acosta, O., & Weist, M.D. (2004). Responses to terrorism: The voices of two communities speak out. In C.S. Clauss-Ehlers & M.D. Weist (Eds.), *Community planning to foster resilience in children* (pp. 143-159). New York, NY: Kluwer Academic Publishers.

Herman, J.L. (1997). *Trauma and recovery: The aftermath of violence--from domestic abuse to political terror.* New York, NY: Basic Books.

Johnson, K. (1998). *Trauma in the lives of children: Crisis and stress management techniques for counselors, teachers, and other professionals.* Alameda, CA: Hunter House Publishers.

Monahon, C. (1997). *Children and trauma: A guide for parents and professionals.* Indianapolis, IN: Jossey-Bass.

vanderKolk, B.A., McFarlane, A.C., & Weisaeth, L. (Eds.), *Traumatic stress: The effects of overwhelming experience on mind, body, and society.* New York, NY: The Guilford Press.

CHAPTER 14. EXCEPTIONAL MICROCULTURES: YOUTH WITH EMOTIONAL DISTRUBANCE- CHILDHOOD DEPRESSION, EATING DISORDERS

Merrell, K.W. (2001). *Helping students overcome depression and anxiety: A practical guide.* New York, NY: The Guilford Press.

Miller, J.A. (1999). *The childhood depression sourcebook.* Columbus, OH: McGraw Hill.

Stark, K.D. (1990). *Childhood depression: School-based intervention.* New York, NY: The Guilford Press.

Teachman, B.A., Schwartz, M.B., Gordic, B.S., & Coyle, B.S. (2003). *Helping your child overcome an eating disorder: What you can do at home.* Oakland, CA: New Harbinger Publications, Inc.

CHAPTER 15. EXCEPTIONAL MICROCULTURES: HOW TO MAKE A REFERRAL

VanDerHeyden, A.M. (2003). Development and validation of a process for screening referrals to special education. *School Psychology Review, 32*(2), 204-228.

SECTION 6. CONCLUSION

CHAPTER 16. CONCLUSION: THE MULTICULTURAL EDUCATOR

Campbell, D.E. (2004). *Choosing democracy: A practical guide to multicultural education* (3rd ed.). Upper Saddle River, NJ: Pearson Education, Inc.

Rhodes, J.E. (1994). Older and wiser: Mentoring relationships in childhood and adolescence. *Journal of Primary Prevention, 14* (3), 187-196.

Sheets, R.H. (2005). *Examining the role of culture in the teaching-learning process.* Boston, MA: Pearson Education, Inc.

Spring, J. (2000). *The intersection of cultures: Multicultural education in the United States and the global economy.* Boston, MA: McGraw Hill.

Glossary of Terms

Androgyny Gender identification that incorporates both masculine and feminine traits.

Anorexia nervosa Clinical course characterized by someone who refuses to maintain a minimally healthy body weight, intensely fears gaining weight, and views self as overweight despite being abnormally thin. Self-image and self-evaluation are largely influenced by one's body-thin ideal. *Source:* American Psychiatric Association (1994). *Diagnostic and statistical manual of mental disorders* (4th ed.). Washington, DC: Author.

Behavioral management As it relates to the classroom, behaviors the teacher implements to negotiate classroom community so that student learning is optimized.

Bem sex role inventory (BSRI) Developed by psychologist Sandra Bem. A sixty-item instrument that assesses gender role identity using feminine, masculine, and neutral or androgynous personality traits.

Bilingual education Using two languages for instructional purposes. The goal is to help children learn in language of origin and reinforce learning through use of a second language like English. *Source:* Gollnick, D.M., & Chinn, P.C. (2002). *Multicultural education in a pluralistic society* (6th ed.). Upper Saddle River, NJ: Merrill Prentice Hall.

Binge eating Symptom that is characteristic of bulimia where the individual eats an unusually high amount of food in a short period of time. The individual often experiences a loss of control during binge eating behavior. *Source:* American Psychiatric Association (1994). *Diagnostic and statistical manual of mental disorders* (4th ed.). Washington, DC: Author.

Bipolar disorder Clinical course characterized by extreme shifts in mood that vacillate between episodes of depression and mania.

Bisexual An individual who is attracted physically and emotionally to people of the same and different genders. *Source:* Lesbian, gay, bi, trans, youth line (n.d.). *Definitions.* Retrieved April 11, 2005, from http://www.youthline.ca/definitions/sexuality.html

Black racial identity development Theory of racial identity development where each Black racial identity status represents a unique worldview that characterizes the individual's cognitive schema about themselves and their world. The four statuses that make up Black racial identity development are: Preencounter, Encounter, Immersion/Emersion, and Internalization. *Source:* Helms, J.E. (1986). Expanding racial identity theory to cover counseling process. *Journal of Counseling Psychology, 33*(1), 62-64.

Bulimia nervosa Clinical course characterized by binge eating and inappropriate compensatory methods to prevent weight gain. *Source:* American Psychiatric Association (1994). *Diagnostic and statistical manual of mental disorders* (4th ed.). Washington, DC: Author.

Bully An individual who repeatedly says or does hurtful things to another person who has problems defending him or herself. Direct attacks and indirect attacks are two types of bullying behaviors. *Source:* United States Department of Health and Human Services. (2003). *Bullying is not a fact of life.* Washington, DC: Author.

Bystander Individual who watches the interaction between bully and victim. Contributes to the bully's sense of power and control, can get a thrill by watching bullying behavior, or is too afraid to get involved. The bystander can influence bullying outcomes by intervening to stop bullying behavior.

Charter schools Offer a publicly funded alternative school education that includes a different curriculum, teaching style, and method of assessment. They are independent of the public school system and have programs geared to meet the needs of the community where they reside.

Child abuse Encompasses physical, sexual, emotional/psychological abuse and neglect and has far-reaching physical, psychological, and behavioral consequences that effect the development of infants, children, and adolescents.

Classroom management Goes beyond classroom discipline and refers to a broad scope of educational practice that includes academic environment, teaching strategies, and overall class structure.

Context-dependent communication Going beyond the spoken word and incorporating larger contextual factors in interpretations of what is being communicated (i.e., the emotion and physical movement associated with the message).

Cultural engagement The importance of engaging families in a manner that reflects their cultural background. *Source:* Tseng, W.S., & Hsu, J.L. (1991). Culture and family assessment. In W.S. Tseng & J.L. Hsu (Eds.), *Culture and family: Problems and therapy* (pp. 171-191). New York, NY: Haworth Press.

Cultural racism Dimension of racism where societal views about some beliefs are considered more important than others. Can be expressed in aesthetics (i.e., how the culture defines beauty), valuing certain art forms above others (i.e., certain types of music), and favoring particular philosophical orientations. *Source:* Jones, J.M. (1981). The concept of racism and its changing reality. In B.P. Bowser & R.G. Hunt (Eds.), *Impacts of racism on White Americans* (pp. 27-49). Thousand Oaks, CA: Sage Publications.

Cultural values Cultural patterns that characterize how we operate. Although often out of our awareness, they influence individual behavior and group norms.

Culture Common heritage or set of beliefs, norms, and values. It refers to the shared and largely learned attributes of a group of people. *Source:* United States Department of Health and Human Services (2001). *Mental health: Culture, race, and ethnicity—A supplement to Mental health: A report of the Surgeon General.* Rockville, MD: U.S. Department of Health and Human Services, Public Health Service, Office of the Surgeon General.

Development Predictable physical, mental, and social changes in life in relation to one's environment. *Source:* Gladding, S.T. (2002) *Family therapy: History, theory, and practice* (3rd ed.). Upper Saddle River, NJ: Merrill Prentice Hall.

Difference An experience of being dissimilar or distinct. Two objectives for understanding difference are to understand the complexity associated with the concept of difference and to develop empathy for differences across a multitude of dimensions.

Dimensions of microcultural difference Cultural groups with shared cultural patterns and similarities. Being from the same microculture, however, does not always imply sameness.

Dysthymic disorder Clinical course characterized by a chronically depressed mood that can be ongoing over the course of many years. *Source:* American Psychiatric Association (1994). *Diagnostic and statistical manual of mental disorders* (4ᵗʰ ed.). Washington, DC: Author.

Emotional abuse Abuse that aims to decrease self-esteem and/or attempts to inflict fear through intimidation.

English as a second language (ESL) programs Language programs that only use English for teaching and instruction. The goal of ESL programs is to have participants become fluent in English as soon as possible.

English language learners (ELL) Individuals whose first language is not English.

Ethnic identity development The process by which an individual develops a sense of self as a member of an ethnic group. According to Phinney's theory, ethnic identity encompasses a three stage process: Stage One, Unexamined Ethnic Identity; Stage Two, Ethnic Identity Search/Moratorium; and Stage Three, Ethnic Identity Achievement. *Source:* Phinney, J.S. (1990). Ethnic identity in adolescents and adults: Review of research. *Psychological Bulletin, 108*(3), 499-514.

Ethnicity A shared cultural heritage that reflects similarity in language, history, and customs transmitted from one generation to the next and reflects a shared national or religious identity. *Source:* United States Department of Health and Human Services (2001). *Mental health: Culture, race, and ethnicity—A supplement to Mental health: A report of the Surgeon General.* Rockville, MD: U.S. Department of Health and Human Services, Public Health Service, Office of the Surgeon General.

Family People who are biologically and/or psychologically related who share a household and have historical, emotional, and/or financial ties. *Source:* Gladding, S.T. (2002) *Family therapy: History, theory, and practice* (3rd ed.). Upper Saddle River, NJ: Merrill Prentice Hall.

Gay Usually refers to men who form physical and emotional relationships with other men although the term can refer to both men and women (i.e., the gay community). *Source:* Lesbian, gay, bi, trans, youth line (n.d.). *Definitions.* Retrieved April 11, 2005, from http://www.youthline.ca/definitions/sexuality.html

Gender One's status as male or female. Has social significance in that boys and girls, men and women, take on roles that are based on the manner in which a culture or society perceives masculinity and femininity.

Gender bias Gaps in educational resources, attainment, performance, and access that are determined by gender.

Gender identity Identity based upon assumed behaviors, attitudes, and feelings tied to the experience of being male or female. Traditional gender identification for boys has focused on independence and achievement. Traditional gender identity among girls has focused on nurturance and passivity.

Gender role Roles that develop from the ways in which males and females are socialized into their gender group.

Herman grid An optical illusion that consists of black squares, white lines, and perceived gray dots. It provides an example of how individuals see, perceive, believe, and act on things in the environment that may not actually exist.

Homophobia An irrational fear or hatred of same-sex attractions expressed through prejudice, discrimination, harassment or acts of violence. *Source:* Lesbian, gay, bi, trans, youth line (n.d.). *Definitions.* Retrieved April 11, 2005, from http://www.youthline.ca/definitions/sexuality.html

Homosexual Someone who is physically and emotionally attracted to people of the same gender. *Source:* Lesbian, gay, bi, trans, youth line (n.d.). *Definitions.* Retrieved April 11, 2005, from http://www.youthline.ca/definitions/sexuality.html

Inappropriate compensatory behaviors Behaviors the individual engages in to counteract the effect of binge eating to prevent weight gain. Examples of methods used to compensate for binge eating include vomiting, diet pills, laxatives, fasting, and extreme exercise. *Source:* American Psychiatric Association (1994). *Diagnostic and statistical manual of mental disorders* (4th ed.). Washington, DC: Author.

Individual racism A behavior or attitude expressed by one individual towards another based on the notion of White superiority and the inferiority of other racial/ethnic groups on an individual basis. *Source:* Jones, J.M. (1981). The concept of racism and its changing reality. In B.P. Bowser & R.G. Hunt (Eds.), *Impacts of racism on White Americans* (pp. 27-49). Thousand Oaks, CA: Sage Publications.

Institutional racism Institutions, such as housing, education, labor, and other quality of life variables that limit the resources, choices, and mobility of different groups of individuals on a racial basis. *Source:* Jones, J.M. (1981). The concept of racism and its changing reality. In B.P. Bowser & R.G. Hunt (Eds.), *Impacts of racism on White Americans* (pp. 27-49). Thousand Oaks, CA: Sage Publications.

Lesbian A woman who is physically and emotionally attracted to other women. *Source:* Lesbian, gay, bi, trans, youth line (n.d.). *Definitions.* Retrieved April 11, 2005, from http://www.youthline.ca/definitions/sexuality.html

Magnet schools Publicly funded elementary, middle, and high schools that specialize in content areas such as academics, science, the fine arts, performing arts, or the humanities and draw students from the surrounding geographical region.

Maintenance approach to bilingual education Approach to bilingual education that promotes student functioning in language of origin and English. The approach proposes that the student become both bilingual and bicultural, with neither culture nor language taking priority. *Source:* Gollnick, D.M., & Chinn, P.C. (2002). *Multicultural education in a pluralistic society* (6th ed.). Upper Saddle River, NJ: Merrill Prentice Hall.

Major depressive disorder Clinical course characterized by a unipolar depression where the individual persistently experiences low mood and sadness. *Source:* American Psychiatric Association (1994). *Diagnostic and statistical manual of mental disorders* (4th ed.). Washington, DC: Author.

Mandated reporter Those required by law to report child abuse and neglect.

Multicultural education Approach to education that values difference and pluralism among students. This educational approach adheres to principles of social justice, anti-discriminatory practices, and the provision of an equitable education for diverse students.

Multiethnic curriculum An educational approach where classroom materials and curriculum incorporate diversity in classroom teachings and interactions throughout course content offerings. Materials, projects, content, and instruction do not solely reflect the dominant culture.

Multicultural educator An educator who is committed to valuing diversity and pluralism among students as evidenced through student interaction, school-wide policies, curriculum development, and instruction that reflects diverse, non-discriminatory behaviors and materials. Professional aim towards self-awareness, flexibility, community-building, advocacy, and ongoing learning about self and others.

National Association of School Psychologists (NASP) Organization that represents and supports school psychology through leadership to enhance the mental health and educational competence of all children. The organization promotes inclusive educational environments.

Neglect Form of child abuse in which the caregiver of a child under the age of 18 has not provided the child with the basic care necessary for adequate growth and development. Neglect also pertains to inadequate supervision of the child. *Source:* Safe Child Program (n.d.). *Safe child: Child abuse.* Retrieved April 6, 2005, from http://www.safechild.org/index.htm

Physical abuse With regard to children, abusive behaviors that involve the physical maltreatment of a child under the age of 18 by a caregiver. *Source:* Safe Child Program (n.d.). *Safe child: Child abuse.* Retrieved April 6, 2005, from http://www.safechild.org/index.htm

Post traumatic stress disorder (PTSD) Chronic and ongoing difficulties related to trauma that are characterized by re-experiencing the trauma, avoiding anything associated with the trauma, and ongoing symptoms of increased arousal not present before the trauma. *Source:* American

Psychiatric Association (1994). *Diagnostic and statistical manual of mental disorders* (4th ed.). Washington, DC: Author.

Prejudice To prejudge someone, or make assumptions about them based on previous experiences, learned stereotypes, and internalized belief systems.

Questioning Individual who is uncertain about his or her sexual orientation.

Race Individuals commonly consider race to be a biological term that defines and categorizes people according to their biological traits. While race as a biological variable has largely been refuted, the concept of race has social meaning. There are social implications that we attach to physical features such as skin color that influence how we view others. Hence, societies like the U.S. classify people into social groups based on characteristics that have social significance. *Source:* U.S. Department of Health and Human Services (2001). *Mental health: Culture, race, and ethnicity—A supplement to Mental health: A report of the Surgeon General.* Rockville, MD: U.S. Department of Health and Human Services, Public Health Service, Office of the Surgeon General.

Racial identity development Development that refers to the individual's psychological orientation to his or her race.

Racism The belief and assumption of superiority of one race over other races. Racism can occur on individual, cultural, and institutional levels.

Referral With regard to a possible mental health problem, to direct a student to a service or service provider for evaluation because of observable behaviors that indicate a potential mental health problem and the need for intervention. Parental involvement and communication with school administrators are part of the referral process.

Rosenthal expectation effect Developed out of an experiment conducted by Robert Rosenthal that was based on the premise that teacher expectations influence student outcomes. The experiment demonstrated that students with teachers who expect them to do well perform better than students whose teachers do not have positive expectations of them.

School choice An educational reform that lets parents decide what school they want their children to attend. School choice gives families and students the opportunity to select publicly funded alternatives to traditional neighborhood schools.

Sexual abuse Any sexual contact with a child or the use of a child for the sexual pleasure of someone else. *Source:* Safe Child Program (n.d.). *Safe child: Child abuse.* Retrieved April 6, 2005, from http://www.safechild.org/index.htm

Sexual orientation development Varying degrees of emotional, romantic, or sexual attraction that develop across one's lifetime. *Source:* American Psychological Association (n.d.). *Just the facts about sexual orientation and youth: A primer for principals, educators and school personnel.* Retrieved April 11, 2005, from http://www.apa.org/pi/lgbc/publications/justthefacts.html

Sign language Vocal sounds and nonverbal communication that have a grammatical structure, syntax, and vocabulary. *Source:* Gollnick, D.M., & Chinn, P.C. (2002). *Multicultural education in a pluralistic society* (6th ed.). Upper Saddle River, NJ: Merrill Prentice Hall.

Socio-economic status (SES) Social and governmental stratification system based on financial differences. A measure of an individual's position on an economic hierarchy that implies mobility to different levels. SES is usually based on income, occupation, and educational attainment.

Stigma An abstract concept that involves misperceptions of those with mental illnesses that are characterized by painful, destructive, discriminatory attitudes and behaviors.

Transgender Self-identifying term for someone whose gender identity or expression differs from traditional gender roles. Refers to someone who crosses gender roles in some way. *Source:* Lesbian, gay, bi, trans, youth line (n.d.). *Definitions.* Retrieved April 11, 2005, from http://www.youthline.ca/definitions/sexuality.html

Transitional approach to bilingual education An assimilationist approach that says bilingual education should be used to have the student shift from the language used at home to the predominant language used in the culture. Maintaining the language of origin is not a priority in this approach. *Source:* Gollnick, D.M., & Chinn, P.C. (2002). *Multicultural education in a pluralistic society* (6th ed.). Upper Saddle River, NJ: Merrill Prentice Hall.

Trauma The experience of external (physical) and internal (emotional or mental) threats that lead to feelings of helplessness in one's ability to be protected by self or others. *Source:* Pynoos, R.S., Steinberg, A.M., & Goenjian, A. (1996). Traumatic stress in childhood and adolescence: Recent developments and current controversies. In B.A. vanderKolk, A. C. McFarlane & L. Weisaeth (Eds.), *Traumatic stress: The effects of overwhelming experience on mind, body, and society* (pp. 331-358). New York, NY: The Guilford Press.

Verbal dependent communication Communication that is based on the verbal words stated by the individual. Tone, emotion, and physical cues are not considered in the interpretation of what is stated.

Victim of bullying The individual who is the recipient of the bully's behavior. Victims may become depressed, feel hopeless, or suffer from low self-esteem due to the bullying behavior.

White racial identity development Differing psychological orientations to race among White individuals. The two-phase process of White racial identity development involves abandoning racism in the first phase (i.e., Contact, Disintegration, and Reintegration statuses) and defining a positive White identity in the second phase (i.e., Pseudo-Independent, Immersion/Emersion, and Autonomy statuses).

Worldview The individual's perception of their relationship to the world including the person's values, beliefs, and assumptions. *Source:* Sue, D. (1981). *Counseling the culturally different: Theory and practice.* New York, NY: Wiley.

Appendix A
Sample Course Syllabus

COURSE DESCRIPTION

Demographic changes mean that contemporary U.S. classrooms are becoming increasingly diverse. Despite such rapid change, many educational systems continue to miss the meaning and importance of teaching within a multicultural framework. The "business as usual" approach too often assumes that all students learn, process information, and approach academic material in the same way. Lost in this assumption are the larger historical, cultural, relational, economic, and political realities that influence a student's cognitive, emotional, and social development.

The purpose of this course is to enhance your ability to identify, grapple with, and ultimately grasp a sense of what is meant by the term difference within educational systems. Through greater awareness and understanding about your own identification with dimensions of difference (i.e., culture, race, ethnicity, gender, and socioeconomic status) you will be better able to understand the diverse life experiences of the children, adolescents, and families who participate in the life of your school.

Additionally, there are many issues that you will have to manage as an educator. Trauma, child abuse, depression, eating disorders, and bullying are a few contemporary problems that have a profound impact on schools. Despite their prevalence, teachers are often at a loss as to how these issues should be addressed when they arise in the classroom. This course seeks to fill these gaps in knowledge through reading, discussion, and skill-building activities. The overall goal of the course is to develop a repertoire of skills to effectively manage these realities.

COURSE OBJECTIVES

1. To increase professional and personal self-awareness and knowledge about diversity.

2. To increase knowledge of societal and psychological barriers that prevent educational success for teachers and students.
3. To develop skills that have a positive impact on student learning and development in a pluralistic society.

CLASS FORMAT

The course is experiential and didactic with lecture and skill-building activities offered throughout. Each class session will provide a lecture that covers the topic for the week (See course schedule). The lecture component consists of didactic information related to assigned readings and selected topics in multicultural education. Skill-building activities involve role-plays, interviews, personal reflection activities, case discussions, and application of the theory through in-class exercises. The course is interactive so that students have the opportunity to discuss their reactions to readings, lectures, and participate in classroom activities.

REQUIRED READING

Clauss-Ehlers, C.S. (2006). *Diversity training for classroom teaching: A manual for students and educators.* New York, NY: Springer.

See the bibliography of selected titles and *Diversity Training Activities* in the text for additional readings.

COURSE REQUIREMENTS/EVALUATION

1. **Midterm Exam.** A midterm exam will be given halfway through the course. *The midterm is worth 40 points.*
2. **Educational intervention proposal paper.** Write an educational intervention paper that proposes a specific intervention that can be implemented in a school setting. You will be assigned groups and write a 15-page paper that spells out the specific educational problem and your proposed intervention. There will be a separate handout for this exercise (See Appendix B) but questions to consider include: How will this intervention differ for different student populations? What are the strengths and weaknesses for addressing the educational issue using your intervention? What other interventions did you consider? How did you choose this one? How does your project relate to the material presented in class? *The paper is worth 40 points* (all students in the group will receive the same grade).

3. **Presentation of educational intervention paper.** Your group will present your intervention to the class and teach your peers about its application. Groups must be prepared to take questions from the class. *The presentation is worth 10 points* (all students in the group will receive the same grade).
4. **Class participation.** You will further enhance your learning of course material by sharing your perspectives and experiences. Class participation will be measured by: 1) attendance, 2) in class comments, 3) demonstrated knowledge of readings, and 4) skill development through participation in *Diversity Training Activities. Class participation is worth 10 points.*

Your final grade will be calculated from the total number of points in these areas.

COURSE SCHEDULE AND READINGS

WEEK 1   INTRODUCTION/ COURSE OVERVIEW
Clauss-Ehlers, Chapter 1.

WEEK 2   HOW DO WE UNDERSTAND DIFFERENCE?
Clauss-Ehlers, Chapter 2.

WEEK 3   CULTURAL VALUES AND WORLDVIEW
Clauss-Ehlers, Chapter 3.

Phinney, J.S. (1996). When we talk about American ethnic groups, what do we mean? *American Psychologist, 51* (9), 918-927.

WEEK 4   SOCIOECONOMIC STATUS
Clauss-Ehlers, Chapter 4.

WEEK 5   RACE & ETHNICITY
Clauss-Ehlers, Chapter 5.

Helms. J. (1994). Racial identity in the school environment. In P. Pedersen & J.C. Carey (Eds.), *Multicultural counseling in schools: A practical handbook* (pp. 19-38). Boston, MA: Allyn & Bacon.

WEEK 6   LANGUAGE IN THE CLASSROOM
Clauss-Ehlers, Chapter 6.

Clauss, C.S. (1998). Language: The unspoken variable in psychotherapy practice. *Psychotherapy, 35* (2), 188-196.

LaFromboise, T., Colman, H.L.K., & Gerton, T. (1993). Psychological impact of biculturalism: Evidence and theory. *Psychological Bulletin, 114* (3), 395-412.

WEEK 7   WORKING WITH DIVERSE FAMILIES: PARENTAL PARTNERSHIP IN EDUCATION
Clauss-Ehlers, Chapter 7.

Eccles, J.S., Midgley, C., Wigfield, A., Buchanan, M., Reuman, D., Flanagan, C., & MacIver, D. (1993). Development during adolescence: The impact of stage-environment fit on young adolescents' experiences in schools and in families. *American Psychologist, 48*(2), 90-101.

Tseng, W.S., & Hsu, J.L. (1991). Culture and family assessment. In W.S. Tseng & J.L. Hsu (Eds.), *Culture and family: Problems and therapy (*pp. 171-191). New York, NY: Haworth Press.

WEEK 8   MIDTERM EXAMINATION

WEEK 9   GENDER
Clauss-Ehlers, Chapter 8.

WEEK 10   SEXUAL ORIENTATION AND YOUTH
Clauss-Ehlers, Chapter 9.

Anderson, D.A. (1994). Lesbian and gay adolescents: Social and developmental considerations. *The High School Journal, 77*, 13-19.

Reynolds, A.L., & Koski, M.J. (1994). Lesbian, gay and bisexual teens and the school counselor: Building alliances. *The High School Journal, 77*, 88-94.

WEEK 11   BULLYING IN SCHOOLS & CLASSROOM MANAGEMENT
Clauss-Ehlers, Chapter 10.

Clauss-Ehlers, Chapter 11.

Ruben, A.M. (1989). Preventing school dropouts through classroom guidance. *Elementary School Guidance and Counseling, 24,* 21-29.

WEEK 12   CHILD ABUSE & RESILIENCE
Clauss-Ehlers, Chapter 12.

Clauss-Ehlers, C. S. (2004). Re-Inventing resilience: A model of "culturally-focused resilient adaptation." In C.S. Clauss-Ehlers & M. D. Weist (Eds.), *Community planning to foster resilience in children* (pp. 27-41). New York, NY: Kluwer Academic Publishers.

Lynch, M., & Cicchetti, D. (1997). Children's relationships with adults and peers: An examination of elementary and junior high school students. *Journal of School Psychology, 35*(1), 81-99.

Pianta, R.C., & Walsh, D.J. (1998). Applying the construct of resilience in schools: Cautions from a developmental systems perspective. *School Psychology Review, 27* (3), 407-417.

WEEK 13   EXCEPTIONAL MICROCULTURES:
DEALING WITH TRAUMA
Clauss-Ehlers, Chapter 13.

Educational Intervention Proposal Papers due.

WEEK 14   EXCEPTIONAL MICROCULTURES:
INDIVIDUALS WITH EMOTIONAL DISTURBANCE:
CHILDHOOD DEPRESSION, EATING DISORDERS
Clauss-Ehlers, Chapter 14.

Presentation of Educational Intervention Proposal Papers.

WEEK 15   EXCEPTIONAL MICROCULTURES:
HOW TO MAKE A REFERRAL
Clauss-Ehlers, Chapter 15.

Presentation of Educational Intervention Proposal Papers.

WEEK 16   CONCLUSION:
THE MULTICULTURAL EDUCATOR
Clauss-Ehlers, Chapter 16.

Presentation of Educational Intervention Proposal Papers.

Appendix B
Educational Intervention Proposal Paper

RATIONALE

The purpose of this paper is to write about an educational intervention that addresses a specific problem in a school setting. The outline for the paper incorporates information that is required for grant applications. In this way you are also learning about the grant writing process.

ASSIGNMENT

Your instructor will pass around a sheet where you will indicate the grade range (i.e., elementary, middle, or high school) that you want your proposal paper to address. Your instructor will then create groups based on your shared interest in grade levels. Each group will consist of 4 to 5 students. Groups will write a 15-page paper that spells out a specific educational problem and your proposed intervention. The intervention can occur on any level: the classroom, an entire grade, or for a school community. Your intervention can involve a lesson plan or some other proposed project. Three important things to consider are:

- an introduction to a problem that the class or school is facing;
- an intervention addressing the problem; and
- an integration of readings and theories throughout your proposal.

Questions to keep in mind as you write your paper are: How will this intervention differ for different student populations? What strengths and weaknesses does your intervention present when addressing the educational issue that your group has selected? What other interventions did your group consider? How did you choose this particular problem? How does your project relate to the material presented in class?

PAPER OUTLINE

The following outline will help your group organize your proposal paper. It is suggested that you provide subtitles for separate sections of your paper with the headings mentioned below. This format will also help group members decide who is going to write about each section of the paper.

1. **Area of Need:** What is the specific problem or need in your classroom or school?
2. **Target Population:** Who is the intervention for? What students are you trying to target?
3. **Criteria for Participants:** Now that you have targeted who the intervention is for, what criteria must students meet to be eligible to participate in your program? If you design a program focused on bullying prevention, for instance, will all students participate or just those who are known to be bullies?
4. **Describe Your Intervention:** Here you will map out the specific intervention that you propose to implement in the school setting. This section presents a full description of your educational program and how you plan to carry it out.
5. **Procedures Needed to Implement Your Proposal:** This section spells out what you need to make your program work. What are the specific procedures that are going to make your intervention effective? Clarify the description of your intervention discussed in point 4.
6. **Rationale for Intervention:** How do you justify your intervention? Incorporate literature that highlights the importance of your intervention. Create a strong argument about why your program is needed in school. For example, the high incidence of school bullying documented in the literature justifies the need for your bullying prevention program.
7. **History Relevant to the Intervention:** Review the literature and discuss existing interventions that address the same issue as yours. What is the history of these programs? What is their success level? What will your program offer that has not been offered before?
8. **Troubleshoot Obstacles to Implementation:** Anticipate and discuss barriers that you expect to get in the way of successfully implementing your intervention. For instance, if you implement a program for students who suffer from depression, will issues of confidentiality and stigma interfere with student readiness to seek services?
9. **Conclusion:** Tie your ideas together in a coherent summary. Remember not to rush through the conclusion. This section provides the opportunity to highlight and review those key points that make your intervention memorable.

PRESENTATION OF EDUCATIONAL INTERVENTION PAPER

Your group will present your intervention to the class and teach your peers about its relevance and application. The following recommendations are geared to help you plan your presentation:

- You have 20 minutes to present your proposal. Presentations will be scheduled over three class times as noted in your course syllabus.
- Each group member must participate in the presentation and present at least one section. This prevents some students from doing all the presenting.
- Reserve 5 minutes at the end of your presentation for questions. This allows you to practice how you will argue for your proposal to a potential funding source.
- Be creative. Bring in handouts, video clips, transparencies—any tool necessary to help you communicate what you'd like the class to understand about your intervention.
- This is your moment to teach--- Have fun!

Index

LaVergne, TN USA
03 September 2009

156927LV00002B/85/A